HOW
A
WRITER
WORKS

HOW A WRITER WORKS

Revised Edition

ROGER GARRISON
Late, Westbrook College

1817

HARPER & ROW, PUBLISHERS, New York
Cambridge, Philadelphia, San Francisco, London,
Mexico City, São Paulo, Singapore, Sydney

Sponsoring Editor: Phillip Leininger
Project Editor: Nora Helfgott
Text and Cover Design: Barbara Bert
Production: Delia Tedoff
Compositor: Donnelley/Rocappi

How a Writer Works, *Revised Edition*

Library of Congress Cataloging in Publication Data
Garrison, Roger H.
    How a writer works.

    Includes index.
    1. English language—Rhetoric.   I. Title.
PE1408.G34   1985 808′.042   84–25236
ISBN 0-06-042242-4

87 88 89 9 8 7 6 5 4 3

For
Essie, dear friend
David, beloved growing son

Both eager learners

Contents

Preface

More often than not, a textbook is someone else's course. This little book is not a course. It is a guide to the process of writing. The emphasis here is on how writing is done, not on its product.

The book assumes that each writer has individual problems—problems all of which cannot be effectively addressed in a class group. Some beginning writers may range from illiteracy to minimum mediocrity; others may range from competence to surprising fluency. Writers' problems vary in degree, not in kind. Whatever their abilities, writers must go through a similar process to say clearly what they want to say.

This book also assumes that the job of teachers of writing is to match problems in expression with learning tasks that are appropriate to their students' levels of skill. It is the instructor's job to determine where each student *begins* and then to guide the student through the making of a piece of writing.

Though it is brief, this is a *demanding* book. It assumes flexibility, imagination, and a certain spontaneity in the relationship between student and teacher. It also assumes a significant measure of direct, person-to-person student-teacher collaboration, very much like the way a professional writer works with an editor. This is the apprentice system updated; it is the way that crafts have been learned for centuries. The book assumes a master (teacher) relationship to the apprentice (beginning writer). In so doing, it may be "radical" only in the sense that it changes the pedagogue-disciple relationship to something more realistic—and incomparably more effective.

The Instructor's Manual that accompanies this text (*One-to-One: Making Writing Instruction Effective*) spells out this relationship in detail: how it works, how it can be adapted or modified to fit particular institutional requirements or student loads. Increasing numbers of teachers in high schools and in colleges are finding that the approach advocated in this book is both personally and professionally satisfying. The same is true of students who are asked to learn to write this way.

Such individual teaching *can* be done, *is* being done. In no way does the approach dilute the quality of instruction; indeed, it is more rigorous than traditional ways of instruction. There is a small but growing body of research which validates the effectiveness of one-to-one (apprentice-master) instruction. And there is a massive bonus for the teacher, and another for the student, in teaching writing this way. The instructor need no longer take home endless stacks of papers to be evaluated and commented on. And the student comes to see writing as a series of skills that can be mastered, one by one. (The student also has the special experience of having the undiluted attention of the teacher.)

This book can be a supplement to another text, if the instructor wants more full treatment of various aspects of writing. Or it can be used on its own if the instructor wants to create his or her own course, with the book used simply as a guide. Though the book has a chapter on writing tasks, a perceptive and imaginative instructor can find dozens of appropriate "assignments" for students throughout. All of these have deliberately been left open-ended so that both teacher and student can have flexibility of choice.

In the book's first edition, I determined to leave out most of the detailed material usually included in standard rhetoric texts (grammar exercises, prose models, and the rest) and concentrate on the crucial skills of the writing process. This revised edition follows the same aim. But with the helpful suggestions of many people, especially students, some of the sections of the book have been slightly amplified or changed to sharpen explanations and to give student writers additional useful problems of expression to work with.

The truth is that despite structured courses, textbooks, and all the apparatus of formal instruction, *learning to write is largely self-taught.* This is so because no matter how trivial or difficult the subject to be expressed, every writer faces the same internal realities: personal thoughts and feelings, often churning and elusive; a store of information; the need to communicate; and, ultimately, the blank piece of paper which is always silent and resistant.

An instructor cannot "teach answers" to these realities. The essence of a teacher's help is in his or her *response* to what the writer has attempted. If that response comes from a trained sensitivity, the writer can be reassured that "Yes, the reader has no doubt about what you are saying here" or "'From this point on, your reader is confused. This sentence [that phrase, these words] does not follow clearly what you have said before. Can you see why? What possible changes do you need here?" Such response is not prescriptive (do this, do that), but it is, in the long run, more useful because it says, "Here you have communicated with your reader, and here you did not." The reasons for the block, the breakdown, are in *your* mind, *your* words; and your solution is to go back to your internal realities and try to express them once more as you truly mean them or feel them.

Again—always—there are the blank page, the tumbling thoughts, the slippery words. There, again, is the reader needing to understand. Never forget this fact: The reader is your most important teacher.

Learning to write well is no mean achievement. And as every professional knows, good writing must be achieved again and again. Anyone who writes, professionally or not, has to learn eventually to become his or her own critic-editor. Since this book leads a student through successive writing skills, it should help him or her develop editorial judgment for the time when there is no longer a teacher nearby to advise or help.

The book has been written to be read as well as "studied." It suggests rather than prescribes. It assumes a learner who needs to be persuaded as well as instructed. Hence the tone is informal, direct person-to-person. Above all, I hope that what is on these pages *communicates*.

Roger H. Garrison

Publisher's note: Roger Garrison had completed his work on the revised edition of *How a Writer Works* when he died on March 1, 1984, after coronary bypass surgery.

chapter 1

Preliminaries

This is a short book—deliberately. There is just so much to be said about writing: The rest is elaboration and fancywork. If you want to learn to write, *do it.*

What you need to learn is *how* a writer works. The process does not follow a fixed formula. Rather, it is a way of approaching almost any problem in expression so that your words can be shaped into meaning. Unlike the methodical following of a recipe or running a complex machine, writing is exploratory: You're not sure what you want to say until you have tried to say it. By doing the writing, you find out whether you have said what you intend.

The main message of this book is that you learn to write by *writing* and *rewriting.* The subject matter of your writing is less important than your persistent effort to say *something* concretely and clearly. If you need to write half a dozen descriptive paragraphs to begin to learn how to revise, then do that. If you try several how-to explanations or persuasions or analyses, do them until they communicate exactly what you mean. You are learning the way a writer works.

This book has eleven short chapters on the basic elements of the process, in the approximate order most writers follow. The act of writing is not as neatly subdivided as these chapters may suggest. Your mind ranges back and forth, and the steps I outline tend to blur together. But when you want to communicate an idea or information to someone else, you face the same problem every time: What, exactly, do I want to say?

How do I begin? What do I do from there? Chapters 2, 3, and 4 show you the basic process. The next seven chapters talk about specific elements of the process once you have words down on paper.

Two analogies are appropriate here.

Suppose you were a sculptor, and you wanted to make a small clay figure of a man with upraised arms and feet-apart stance. This figure is your "subject." You will make an armature of heavy wire, a kind of stick figure of the skeletal outline of the position you have in mind. Then you scoop handfuls of wet clay from a crock and press these roughly around the armature. (The wet clay is analogous to your fact list, which I describe in Chapter 3.) Then you scrape off excess clay and press and shape the remaining clay until it begins to conform to your inner vision of the figure you want to create. (This is revision—Chapter 4—and what follows that.)

Or think of yourself as a cabinetmaker. You want to make a table, a simple one. First you decide what uses the table will have. Assume that it is a coffee table. You then have limits to your design: length of legs, length and width of tabletop. Next you choose your materials. Suppose you want maple, a close-grained hardwood that can be stained in wonderfully subtle colors. According to your basic design, you make the table. Then, if you are a good craftsman, there are careful finishing steps: rounding corners, perhaps; beveling edges; sanding and sanding until the wood feels like velvet. Finally, the finish: hard wax and lots of rubbing, or a light stain, and then French finish with linseed oil, again rubbing layer after layer, until the color is like dark honey and the wood glows with a muted shine.

These are fair comparisons to the writer's task. The chapters in this book take you through this sequence with words instead of clay or wood.

Chapter 12 presents a number of tasks, increasing in difficulty. These are not assignments in the usual sense. They are open-ended problems in expression, suggestive of a range and variety of kinds of writing.

I have not tried to provide full material for a writing course. The material of such a course comes from what *you* write, or try to write. The first job of any writer, however inexperienced, is to determine what he or she wants to say. *This is the first step in the writing process.* My aim in this book is to help you, once you have made this decision, and to show you what a writer does with an idea or subject.

For this reason, you and your instructor may find it difficult, at first, to use this book as a week-by-week text. I didn't design it to be such a thing, since there are plenty of those available. Rather, I begin where any writer starts: What do I have to say? To whom am I saying it, and for what reasons? So use this book as a guide to wherever you are in the process. If I had given you a series of assignments and had suggested that if you accomplished these in series you would have learned to write, I would have cheated you. What counts is not prescriptions—mine or anyone's—but what is on your mind and what you decide to say. If you have nothing on your mind, no textbook is going to help you much.

This book is shoptalk about a craft. In any craft, shoptalk is a valuable way to learn what you need to know. For forty-five years I have been a working writer. For thirty-five of those years I have taught college freshmen and high school students. For seventeen years, I have taught college English teachers. This experience, to put it lightly, has taught humility. It has also taught some hard lessons, ones that all writers learn if they keep at their craft. These lessons I will try to share with you. If I fail to do this well, the shortcoming is mine. It is in the nature of writing that qualified failure is a constant companion: It comes with the territory.

Throughout, I have used the term *writer* to mean simply "a person who writes." A writer is anyone who communicates thoughts, information, ideas, feelings, or any material from experience, in writing, to others. Whenever you write—whatever you write and for whatever reasons—you *are* a writer.

chapter 2

You Can Learn to Write

In northern New England, where I live, stone walls mark boundaries, border meadows, and march through the woods that grew up around them long ago. Flank-high, the walls are made of granite rocks stripped from fields when pastures were cleared and are used to fence in cattle. These are dry walls, made without mortar, and the stones in them, all shapes and sizes, are fitted to one another with such care that a wall, built a hundred years ago, still runs as straight and solid as it did when people cleared the land.

Writing is much like wall building. The writer fits together separate chunks of meaning to make an understandable statement. Like the old Yankee wall builders, anyone who wants to write well must learn some basic skills, one at a time, to build soundly. This book describes these skills and shows you how to develop them and put them together. You *can* learn them.

Building a stone wall is not easy: It is gut-wrenching labor. Writing is not easy either. It is a complex skill, mainly because it demands a commitment of our own complicated selves. But it is worth learning how to do well—something true of any skill. Solid walls do get built, and good writing does get done. We will clear away some underbrush and get at the job.

First consider what writing is not:

- *Writing is not a series of formulas to follow.* Writing is what you have in your mind to say and your search for the right combinations of words to say it.
- *Writing is not a set of rules.* There are, of course, standards of usage to follow—grammar, syntax, and proper spelling. But these are relatively simple: They reflect clear thinking and are the verbal equivalent of good manners or courtesy.
- *Writing is not a special style or vocabulary.* What we call style is a writer's own voice, a special way of looking at the world and talking about it. This is the intellectual-emotional quality of a *person*, and it comes through when the person writes. You will have a style when you have developed your own point of view.
- *Writing is not the use of special forms.* Depending on its function or purpose, a piece of writing will take a certain form—memo, letter, essay, or whatever—because the form expresses the purpose. You do not learn to write by beginning with "comparison-contrast," "persuasion," "description," or other so-called rhetorical modes. Your writing, if it is honest—*and it always should be honest*—will take a form that best communicates what you try to say.
- *Writing is not completely thought through ahead of time.* You shouldn't hold off writing until you have a detailed outline (in fact, formal outlines tend to stiffen writing). Writing is an *act of discovery*. It is a way of seeking the best information for your intentions and of setting the tone and pace of what you have to say.

Beginning writers are not told often enough, if ever, that writing is a craft and—surprisingly—at first a relatively simple craft. It gets subtly more difficult and frustrating as you make increasingly complex statements. But a journeyman carpenter can develop the skill to be a cabinetmaker, and some cabinetmakers even become artists. Your aim is to write so that your own distinctive voice comes off the page. If a reader says, "That sounds just like you," take it as a first-rate compliment.

Since "finding your own voice" may be a new idea to you, I want to say more about it, briefly. We are all different from each other, though we share a common humanity. We are, as we say, "individuals." Each of us sees reality in a distinctive fashion. George Bernard Shaw, the great British writer, said, "You are the window through which you must see the world." We reflect this awareness when we say of someone else, "Oh, she has *style*"—and I don't mean clothing here. Or perhaps we say of a fine athlete, "He's got real style." Such comments recognize an individuality of character that communicates itself to us strongly, often without words.

E. B. White, one of America's finest writers, said in a letter to a correspondent who had asked about "communication" that "the whole problem is to establish communication with one's self, and, that being done, everyone else is tuned in. In other words, if a writer succeeds in communicating with a reader, I think it is simply because he has been trying (with some success) to get in touch with himself—to clarify the reception."°

There is rarely style without clarity. Any reader's unspoken questions reveal whether the writer is clear or confused. The reader says: "You're telling me about a subject I might be interested in. How good is your information? Are *you* trying to tell it straight and clean? If you are, I'll understand you. I'll recognize an honest communicator behind the words."

The rest of this book tries to show you how to find your own style— your own distinctive voice—and how to *craft* writing to let that voice be heard.

Any craft has both tools and processes that are peculiar to it. Processes and tools are inseparable. The next chapter begins with the basic ones.

°E. B. White, *Letters of E. B. White*, ed. Dorothy Lobrano Guth (New York: Harper & Row, 1976), p. 417.

chapter 3

Writing Is Building

Despite their differences of mind, background, and temperament, most professional writers work through a remarkably similar sequence of *prewriting, writing, revising,* and *editing.*

This sequence implies a clear order of priorities in building a piece of writing, whether for a single paragraph or a ten-page article. It can help you identify what to do first, second, third, and so on.

1. Idea or subject
2. Information (content) } Prewriting
3. Your point of view
4. **Rough draft** (a draft is a first-sketch try)
5. Organization (logical sequence of information) } Revising
6. Sentences (grammar, rhythm, tone) } and
7. Diction (best words, spelling) } editing

You will learn to write more effectively, and more quickly, if you follow this sequence, too. But keep in mind that this sequence is only a guide and that each step of the writing process is likely to blend into the others. Sometimes prewriting will go quickly, but revising may be slow and frustrating. Or the reverse may be true. Much depends on your subject, your grasp of it, and perhaps on the pressure of a deadline.

Three basic demands control your writing: your purposes, your reader, and your attitude toward your subject.

- *Purpose.* Why are you writing? Is it a description, an analysis, a summary of information, a complaint, an argument to persuade? (Suggestion: It often helps before you try a first draft to state your purpose in *one* sentence.)
- *Reader.* Is your writing a response to a teacher's assignment or an employer's demand? Is it to a general audience? Your reader's needs or expectations in each case will be different. Thus the form and tone of your response is an appropriate response to your specific audience.
- *Attitude.* Your own feelings or convictions will influence not only the form of presentation but also the shape and rhythm of sentences and, especially, your choices of words.

Form follows function. This is true in nature, and it is true for writing. Form—the total architecture of a work, no matter how trivial—is the expression of *your* meaning and the way you want it to be received.

1. PREWRITING

Prewriting is everything you do before you try a first draft. The *idea* comes first. What are you going to write about? Generally, inexperienced writers' ideas are too inclusive, like Capital Punishment, Abortion, Divorce, Energy, the Generation Gap, or Politics. Limit your subject, narrow it, focus it. How? One analogy: Think of your whole subject as a large pie, and cut one narrow slice of it. Another analogy: A great movie director said, "A movie is simple. It's just long shots, medium shots, and close-ups. But what's the best mix of these to tell your story? Ah, then it's not so simple." Like a movie, writing is a mix of "shots."

For your first attempts at writing, start with small slices, with close-ups. Try just one paragraph. A paragraph is a single developed unit of meaning. If you learn to write good paragraphs, you can write longer, more complex statements.

Suppose your general subject is energy. One paragraph's thin slice of that large pie could be the British thermal unit (BTU), a standard measurement of heat, or a calorie, a basic "unit" of heat. Plain definition is easy; the dictionary supplies it. But if you want to explain BTU to a reader, you need information.

2. INFORMATION

Information (content) is the second prewriting step, and the most important. You cannot write anything (even poetry) without information. You need facts, details, examples. What is a BTU? How is it used? What are differing BTU values for various fuels? In what ways is a BTU an energy-measurement tool? And so on. You will probably need sources to find facts. Make a list of the facts you need quickly, in any order. Your information list should have at least twice as much as you eventually use. Two writer's truisms: Write from richness. Write more about less.

Make your list substantive (full of facts). A series of vague or general phrases will not help you much. *Making the list is already writing.* Think of it as a bank of raw material on which you will draw.

Here are two brief examples to show how two students handled the problem of focus (cutting a narrow slice of the pie) and of making a fact list for a paragraph on a narrowed-down subject.

Student A

General Subject: Sports

Title: Our Crummy Basketball Team

Fact List:
- Disorganized guys
- Don't care
- Break training all the time
- Cut every practice short
- Coach hasn't good control
- Lots of griping on team
- No school spirit
- Student fans throw beer cans and rubbish on court
- Half-time show terrible. Cheerleaders don't work together
- What's my athletic fee buying?

Student B

General Subject: Energy

Title: A Family Beats Oil Prices

Fact List:
- Ours is eight-room house
- In 1978, burned 1,726 gallons oil @ 49¢
- In 1979–80, 872 gallons @ 98¢
- Difference: insulation, walls, roof cap, two wood stoves
- Cost of insulation and stoves: $1,500
- "Payback" period (when these paid for) estimated two years. Estimated cost
- Five cords hardwood (maple, oak, birch) from own woodlot per year
- 1 cord (4′ × 4′ × 8′) = 200 gallons oil
- Family sweats to cut wood. Callused hands from splitting

Clearly, student A is going to have a problem developing his paragraph. The only specific statement in his list is "Student fans throw beer cans and rubbish on court." The rest of the list is vague: It needs examples or specific facts. He'll have to make another list, maybe three or four more.

Student B, however, obviously speaks from experience, including calluses on the hands. She has facts about the number of gallons of heating oil burned and the rising cost. She knows the equivalent of a cord of hardwood compared to gallons of oil. She is obviously going to do the arithmetic to explain the estimated "payback"—when the investment in insulation and stoves, with the use of wood, is paid off in financial terms.

I have deliberately not printed the two resulting paragraphs for a good reason: I want you to examine carefully the nature of the two lists. *Here* is where you learn to be explicit, and you won't get much good from trying to write a paragraph from a vague list. I'll say it again: Making lists *is* writing. *And* thinking. And trying to make something real come off a page of words.

Alternatives

Many writers discover that instead of making lists, rearranging them, and listing again, an effective way to begin is free writing, or "automatic" writing. The idea is simply to write—anything—for five or ten minutes. Write quickly, without rushing. Don't stop to correct spelling or grammar. Don't stop to look back. If you can't think of a word or phrase, just leave a blank, or write "I can't think of it," and keep going. Continue writing *something,* even if it is nonsense. If you're stuck, write whatever silly phrases pop into your head—including "Dammit, I'm stuck."

Most of what you produce this way won't make sense; it will be garbage. But more often than not, there will be a jewel in that garbage: a phrase or sentence or even a single word that will begin to express what you are struggling to say. Start again, beginning with the meaningful phrase, and free-write for another five minutes, this time trying to keep as close to the starting idea as you can. Once again, leave blanks where you need more information or can't think of appropriate words.

Remember: The typical hesitations, blocks, frustrations, and irritations are most acute in the getting-started phase of the process. (Is that spelled right? Is this grammatical?) Half-formed ideas and feelings spin in your mind. Words slide off your mental tongue.

Don't hesitate. *Get it down. Fast. In any order.* Whatever it is, no matter how mixed up, *get it down*. You are stockpiling raw material for future construction. *Get it down*. I can't give you a more useful piece of advice.

3. YOUR POINT OF VIEW

Once you have your list, you have two key questions to answer: *What* do I want to say about a BTU and *who* is my audience? (If you have no specific audience, write to yourself.) Here is where point of view overlaps with organization. Write half a dozen lead (opening) sentences. Choose the one that comes closest to your intentions. You will probably rewrite it later, but for now, let it stand. Using the lead as a guide, shuffle the separate elements in your list until the sequence of your information seems logical.

4. ROUGH DRAFT

Now write a **rough draft** of your paragraph—quickly. If you can, put the draft away for a few hours—or longer, if your deadline permits ("let it cool off," writers say). When you pick it up again, put yourself in the place of a reader. Reading aloud often helps. Listen first for a logical, sensible order of statements or examples. Put question marks in places that don't "feel" right or seem weak or thin. You may need to return to your original information list for more or different material. This is where *revision* (rewriting) begins. This is cut-and-add time, change-around time. You may want to rewrite your lead here. And you will doubtless rewrite it at least once again as you build closer to a final draft. (Revising and editing will be discussed in more detail in the following chapters.)

Writing Thin

Inexperienced writers are apt to write "thin" at first. They tend to assume that once stated, something is, in fact, completely said or that a generalized assertion is informative enough for a reader. This is rarely so. Readers crave information packed into small, telling details. For example, "He was fat" is vague. "He was obese" is slightly more explicit because the word suggests gross size. "His belly sagged over his belt and his heavy jowls quivered as he spoke" substitutes visual details for the word *fat* and more accurately reflects the writer's intention.

The instinct for detail develops and sharpens with practice. (See Chapter 4 for more on this.)

You will usually find that this step-by-step prewriting and rough draft process has to be repeated—more than once—before you feel in clear control of what you want to say. You "recycle" your ideas and information because you discover that you are not as organized as you thought you were. An almost cliché question pinpoints the problem exactly: "How do I know what I think until I say what I mean?" The question is neither flippant nor foolish; indeed, it reflects a potent *process* of learning.

For example, here is a first draft of a student's brief paragraph (she had chosen her own subject). Read it carefully. For now, don't try to analyze; simply *respond*. Does it *feel* to you as though she has truly said what she meant to say?

An event that changed my life was what happened to me a few weeks ago at the hospital. I was there as a nurse's aid. Well, anyway, this man was brought into the emergency room. He was young. About 25 I think. Well, he was in bad shape because he had a heart attack. Everyone rushed around and they brought in all kinds of equipment and they did all kinds of things to him. A couple of the doctors even swore and made jokes. But he died anyway. Right there. It really scared me to realize that someone could be so young and then just die like that so suddenly. Some people at the hospital don't take their job seriously at all. I think medical people should take their job seriously and realize that what they do is important it can mean the difference between life and death.

For the moment, forget the grammatical errors (there are a few). Has the writer sharply communicated her meaning to you? Or aren't you sure? What, in fact, is the writer's main problem with this paragraph?

Let me take you through this one; then I'll give you another sample to work with on your own.

Primarily, the writer is not sure *what* she wants to say. There are three, perhaps four, ideas, none of which she has developed. (1) "An event that changed my life": Nothing more is said about such a change. (2) "It really scared me to realize . . .": She says no more about *what* scared her. (3) "Some people . . . don't take their job seriously": She doesn't tell what gave her this idea. (4) "Medical people . . . should realize that what they do . . . can mean the difference between life and death." And then she stops.

When the student and I discussed the paragraph, I pointed out her four different statements and asked which one was most vivid or important to her. She said immediately, "I was scared. I'd never seen anybody die before." I said, "That sentence struck me as the most genuine. Tell me—tell a reader—what scared you. What was going on that made it scary?"

She said, "Well, they banged his chest with their fists, and one doctor shoved an enormous needle right into his chest. And then they put a couple of electric paddles against his chest and there was a loud bang and his body jumped up a little on the table. Wow. And one of the nurses swore and pointed at the TV monitor, which had a flat white line on it and was making a thin screeching noise—and . . . and . . . the nurses and doctors just stood there and looked at each other and slumped. Then I realized the man was dead."

I said, "Why don't you make a list of what you have just told me, plus any other details you remember, and then write a draft showing what scared you?"

Her final version, several drafts later, was a vivid narration of a frightening experience. I have deliberately *not* printed it because I wanted you to focus on her first step toward clarifying her real meaning.

The next brief paragraph was a response to an assignment in a retail merchandising class: Tell a reader briefly what comparison shopping is.

Comparison shopping is one way to find out quality and prices. For instance, you go to a speciality shop or booteek, a general high quality department store, a discount place, and a general cheap merchandise place, like K-Mart, and you examine a particerler itum. You check prices in each store. Or same type itum. Then you try and see whether quality matches price, and you try to note down the differences. Or the same with brand names and non brands. Comparison shopping teaches you what to look for, like design, workmanship, practical use, and things like that. I found a great handbag like this once. All in all, comparison shopping will help you stretch your shopping dollars and you sometimes find real bargins and besides its fun.

You're on your own. Rewrite this one, adding any information you wish and making changes wherever you need to. Remember the demand of the assignment.

Inspiration

There is, of course, such a thing. It's a quick flash of an idea; a sudden awareness of a relationship not seen before; a strong yen to express a feeling; or a desire to tell another of a special experience. It is, as a writer friend puts it, "an itch you have to scratch."

But don't count on it. If you say, "I couldn't write anything because I wasn't inspired," you're kidding yourself. Fortunately, inspiration *can* be bidden, like flame from the stirred embers of a nearly dead fire. The act of writing—anything—almost invariably generates ideas, information, insights. The sculptor August Rodin said, "Make something, and the ideas will come." The "making," no matter how fumbling, even aimless at first, will itself be an inspiration.

Remember, don't let lack of inspiration be an excuse; what you are really admitting is lack of will.

Some notion of the difficulty and sophistication of the writing act is reflected in an analogy:°

> Imagine the Writer perched like Humpty-Dumpty on top of a wall. On one side of the wall, imagine a great heap of all the material he wants to write about: facts, happenings, feelings, ideas. On the other side of the wall, facing it, is a Reader. He cannot see what the Writer sees; he can see only the wall. (The Writer can see both sides.) The Writer's job is to select from the welter of material on the opposite side of the wall what he wants his Reader to know and understand; to shape this selection into sequence and sense; to translate the sequence into words, sentences, and paragraphs; and finally to post these on the Reader's side of the wall. These written symbols are all that the Reader can use to make contact with the material from the wall's other side.

°Adapted from a similar analogy by Elizabeth Bowen.

chapter 4

Revision: "Seeing Again"

Writing is learned by writing, and in no other way. No instructor can "teach" you how to write, though he or she can help you learn by being a responsive reader and helpful editor.

Rewriting is the key to good writing. Rewriting you must do alone, since it has to come out of your own head. Revision is your chief writing instructor; you learn to write *as* you write and *re*write.

After prewriting, you do a rough draft—your first try at putting your information together. One writer calls this a "discovery draft," and the term is exactly right. You discover whether you are saying what you mean to say.

Your task is to shape and mold your draft to come as close to your intentions as possible. It would be easy to give you general advice about rewriting. But as Oliver Wendell Holmes once remarked, "No generalization is worth a damn, including this one." There aren't any simple steps or rules. What you have written belongs to you. Any changes or developments also come from you. No book can read your mind or sense your feelings.

If you and I could sit side by side, with your draft between us, I could give you reader responses and reader questions: Does your second point follow your first? Does this sentence mean what you want it to? What does this phrase mean? Is this an accurate word, or can you find a more specific one? But for now, you have only this book in front of you.

What I *can* do, however, is reverse the process and let you into *my* mind as I revise a piece of my own writing. I will share with you exactly my thinking, as nearly as I can reproduce it, as I rewrote a single paragraph. Here is the situation:

I write almost every day, sometimes a line or two, sometimes more. There is always an article or a book in the works. I keep a journal, a workbook where I jot down ideas, bits of experience, thoughts, discussion with myself. The workbook is my personal cultch pile. (*Cultch* is Yankee for discarded odds and ends that may be useful someday; after all, you never know.)

Late in September recently, I visited a friend who lives in New Hampshire's White Mountains. (My own roots, both family and spiritual, are in this spare, hard country.) Her home has been in her family for seven generations. She gave me a room where I could write and where, looking out a window, I could see the mountains in the distance. Occasionally I took a break from my work and simply stared out the window. Inside myself I felt—I did not think in any coherent way—how deeply *home* New Hampshire was, how I responded to autumn, my favorite season, and how, simply, I *belonged* here. In my journal I wrote:

Short break from the drudgery. Out the window, hills are hazy-blue in the sunny afternoon. Big bee, striped yellow and black, fat with nectar from the flowers, bats against the screen. Buzzzzz, stop. Buzzzzz, stop. A lifetime of these Septembers, these beloved autumns; then winters and brief springs and summers; and my God I get a lump in my throat because I can feel my way back to my great-great-grandfather who saw these brooding hills exactly as I see them now, who smelled the cut hay, who heard another bee at the window.

I chose this entry because, as I write this now, I am in the same New Hampshire house on a September day. The journal paragraph is my way of prewriting. I want you, as a reader, to share my feeling of the season, my love for a New England fall. As I revise the entry, I will make notes to myself and to you. I want you to come along with me in the process.

As it is with any writer, there are two characters in my head: the Writer (me) and a Reader/Editor (also me), who represents anyone who reads what I write. These two talk to each other.

Reader's question*	Writer's response
1. What are you going to tell me? What's your point?	1. Opening statement; lead.
2. I'm not sure what you mean.	2. Brief qualification of opening, or perhaps an example.
3. Prove it to me. Show me.	3. Information, examples, details.
4. So what?	4. Summary, conclusion, inclusive example.

*Adapted from Mina Shaughnessy, *Errors and Expectations* (New York: Oxford University Press, 1977).

If you are a beginning writer, you find it hard, at first, even to recognize this Reader, to say nothing of being able to listen to him. But if you cultivate internal listening, your Reader/Editor will begin to show himself as a creative nag who pokes you with questions like "So what?" or "What does that mean?" Think of him as a kind of archaeologist who scrapes and digs beneath the surface of your mind to throw up memories and associations, unearthing what you thought you had forgotten. Then the Editor part of him forces you to see what you *have* written, not what you think you have written. Once you get to know him, this Reader/Editor can be trusted.

You will notice, as you follow the revisions, that the journal entry changes—evolves—into something else. The original entry stressed my sense of continuity with the past. But as I started a draft, I realized that I wanted first to express my feelings about the unfolding of autumn from mid-September to November. If I were to develop the idea of successive generations, it would come in later paragraphs. *Let this changing happen;* it is almost invariably what rewriting does.

Now, back to my journal paragraph.

Reader: What's your point here?
Writer: I want some reader in New Mexico or Nebraska or Oregon, who has never been east—any reader, for that matter—to understand my feelings about a New England autumn.
Reader: Your entry doesn't show me much. A bee at the screen and great-grandfathers. Hazy mountains and sentimental stuff about a lump in the throat—cliché, you know.
Writer: I don't want more than a paragraph. Any more might get sticky.

Reader: So put me in place. Where are you and what are you doing when you have these feelings?

Writer: I'm at a friend's house in New Hampshire in September. I'm writing. When I look out the window, I can see the mountains.

Reader: Show me. Start there, anyway.

Writer: I want a lead to give you a sense of place and a feeling of time—continuity.

Draft lead. I am writing, and my papers are spread out on a 150-year-old trestle table. The rubbed wood is satiny to the touch. When I look up, I see the mountains, blue-hazy in the distance. They are old mountains, not like the raw upthrust western Rockies.

Reader: You're getting off the point. I don't want to see the Rockies. Stick to New Hampshire.

Writer: OK, you're right. I'll come back to it with more detail. I want you to see the color, too.

Reader: Color?

Writer: A regional expression: the changing color of the leaves—spectacular. For a brief time, this is one of the most beautiful spots on earth.

Notes: *Maples and sumac: red-orange; birch and beech, yellow; poplar, gold; oak, leather-brown; hackmatack, lighter green; pines shedding showers of brown needles.*

Reader: Give me more. I've got five senses, after all.

Writer: The changes through fall. November, first sleet, snow.

Notes: *Ground hard as iron. Heavy frost on brown grass and shrubs. Grass crackles under foot. Sight and smell of the root cellar under the house—all that harvest down there.*

Reader: What harvest?
Writer: Wait. I'm beginning to feel a sequence for this thing. I want to move from September to November. I'm going to try another draft, which usually dredges up useful stuff; details, words, phrases often find themselves.

Notes: *Forget bee at window. Forget great-great-grandfather. See, touch, smell, hear.*

SECOND DRAFT

As I write this, my papers are spread out on a 10-foot trestle table made of 2 joined pine boards, each 20 inches wide and 3 inches thick. It's a 150-year-old antique, in constant use all that time. The wood feels satiny under my hand. As I look out the window, I can see ranges of mountains receding in the hazy distance. Already, some trees have turned color: red-orange maples, blazing sumac, golden birch. Nowhere do I feel the procession of seasons more than here. Soon, the ground will freeze hard as iron, and the November snows will come down the valleys. In the root cellar of the old house will be the fruits of the harvest.

Reader: Your organization is getting into shape. But I want more details.
Writer: Yes, it's thin. I'll do another draft. I'm beginning to feel the sentences.

Notes: *List some stuff in the root cellar. Ending?*

THIRD DRAFT

In the next draft, I have underlined added or changed material. The writing is beginning to flow and sentences to take on rhythms. There is a slight overlap into the editing stage. None of this is deliberate—yet. It is occurring because *I am writing my way into it.* I now know what I want to say: the movement from late summer, through fall, to winter's beginning. Now I have to find out how I can say this best. The third draft is still "discovering."

As I write, my papers are spread out on an antique trestle table, made of 2 joined boards, each 20 inches wide and 3 inches thick. Around me are old sideboards, chairs, tables, bookcases, all handmade, sturdy, priceless, with the satiny shine that only rubbed pine can have. Across the long valley, I can see the Presidential and Franconia ranges, and more in the blue-hazy distance. Already some maples and sumac are flaring red-orange, signs of the color when autumn begins to draw its paintbrush across the hills. From mid-September to late October, there is no more beautiful spot on earth. Then, for a brief October period, the color fades and there will be Indian summer, warm and russet-gold, a brief benison. Then the November snows will come down the valleys, and my breath will be white in the morning, and the ground will turn to iron. In the root cellar of the old house will be the smell of apples, of cider in stone jugs, of onions, squash, seed corn hung from the rafters, and potatoes in bins and jars of canned vegetables and all the fall bounty.

Reader: Now you're beginning to tell me something. But it's not right yet. The ending, for instance: It's weak.

Notes: *Earthy smell of potatoes. Dank cellar. Put specific vegetables in jars.*

In the third draft, you see more than added information. You may have noticed that I have begun to cut and change. "Procession of the seasons" is out, for instance; "Indian summer" is added. Such changes are a central part of the process as you dig more and more into your memory and your store of sense impressions. All of us have these resources. The act of writing allows us to get at them.

FOURTH DRAFT

In the fourth draft, I've got hold of what I want to say. My Reader turns Editor, and here is where the changes become calculated. The comments to the left of the draft reflect what that internal Editor thought as I began to polish the paragraph.

Some last cut-or-add editing, sentence cadences, word choices, consistent tense, grammar check.	As I write, my papers are spread ~~out~~ on an antique table made of 2 joined
Plank is more accurate than *board*.	*planks,* ~~boards~~, each 20 inches wide and 3 inches thick. *Around* ~~Surrounding~~ me are old
Chairs—one item too many.	sideboards, ~~chairs~~, tables, bookcases—
Priceless—not needed.	handmade, sturdy, ~~priceless~~, with the
Patina is the right word: suggests both look and feel.	*patina* ~~satiny shine~~ that only rubbed pine can
	have. Across the valley are the
Place names have afterechoes: They resonate, especially in a sequence. Remember Benét's poem about American names. And the line in Thoreau's little poem, "twine, wine, hides, and China teas."	Presidential and Franconia ranges—Mt. Washington, Jefferson, Kinsman, the Nubbles, the Three Graces, and more in
Don't overdo adjectives.	*scoured-down* the ~~blue~~-hazy distance—the ~~rounded~~

Confused. Horizon didn't come from Ice Age. Glaciers rubbed down—scoured—the land.

Harbinger—old usage: herald of royal progress. *Yes.*

Save words.

Rhythm of adjectives.

Benison—wrong tone, archaic. Not snow, *sleet*. (Snow is quiet.) *Come down*—weak. *Hissing*—exactly right sound. *Intervales*—New England term for small valleys.

Smoke—active verb.

Turn to iron—cliché.

Earthy? Winy? Tart?

hills ~~horizon~~ from the last Ice Age. Already

flare ~~some~~ maples and sumac ~~are flaring~~ red-

harbingers orange, ~~forerunner~~ of the color when

autumn draws its paintbrush across the

land. In ~~hills. For a brief~~ late October ~~period,~~ the

color fades, and there is Indian summer,

hazed, hushed, warm, russet-gold, a

blessing. brief ~~benison.~~ Then the November sleet ~~snows~~ comes hissing down the intervales, ~~come down the valleys,~~ and my breath

smokes ~~will be white~~ in the morning, and the muddy ruts in the meadow road stone. ~~ground~~ will turn to ~~iron.~~ In the dank root

cellar of the old house will be the tart

smell of apples, the earthy smell of

potatoes in bins. In stone jugs lining the

walls, cider turns hard. Onions, squash,

Succession of nouns to suggest bounty.

seed corn hang from the rafters; and

long shelves of canned tomatoes, beets,

green beans, zucchini soup, pickles, nut

squash, and peaches are the fall bounty

to stretch winter into May. ~~I have a love~~

Last sentence too sentimental. Cut.

~~affair with New England, and autumn is~~

~~its climax.~~

FIFTH DRAFT

No draft is "final," but this is the last one I am going to do. My purpose has been to take you through a revision process as clearly as I could so that you could see what I have meant by "discovery" and "development."

As I write, my papers are spread on an antique table made of 2 planks, each 20 inches wide and 3 inches thick. Around me are old sideboards, tables, bookcases—handmade, sturdy, with the satin patina that only rubbed pine can have. Across the valley are the Presidential and Franconia ranges—Mt. Washington, Jefferson, Lafayette, Kinsman, the Nubbles, the Three Graces in the hazy distance—the rounded hills scoured down by the last Ice Age. Already maples and sumac flare red-orange, harbingers of the color when autumn draws its paintbrush across the land. In late October, the color fades, and there is Indian summer, warm, hazed, hushed, russet-gold, a brief blessing. Soon the November sleet comes hissing down the intervales, my breath smokes in the morning, and the muddy ruts in the meadow road turn to stone. In the dank root cellar of the old house is the tart smell of apples, the earthy smell of potatoes in bins. In stone jugs lining the walls, cider turns hard. Onions, squash, seed corn hang from the rafters; and long shelves of canned tomatoes, beets, green beans, zucchini soup, pickles, nut squash, and peaches are fall bounty to stretch the winter into May.

Revision or editing is hard work, but it is rewarding. You see and feel meaning develop under your pen or on your typewriter. Even for a beginning writer, there can be mounting excitement. As I rewrote this paragraph, I literally *felt* my way back into the magic of autumn. If you go back to the original journal entry and then through the drafts, you will see the paragraph moving toward the feeling I wanted to communicate. In each draft, I added *substance:* facts, particulars, details. My internal Reader nagged me for more information, packed in. It is for finding these details that rewriting is most valuable. (If you have too many, you can always cut some out.)

There are other changes to make, not so much revision as editing: finding strong verbs (verbs are the muscle of sentences): "sleet *comes hissing* down the intervales" or "my breath *smokes* in the morning," and using adjectives and nouns or phrases that evoke sights, sounds, and smells.

SUGGESTIONS

- When you are in doubt, especially in your first draft, *over*write. Pack in more than you think you need. Continue to make notes of added details that come to mind. It is easier to cut than to add. Not having enough information is a problem for any writer, especially an inexperienced one. Most persons, until they accept the need to rewrite, tend to write "thin" and try to get by with a first, underdeveloped draft.
- Give yourself the physical means for experimenting. Use standard 8½-by-11-inch paper; smaller sheets are hard to handle. Write on every other line of a lined page; if you type, use double or triple spacing. Leave wide margins so you'll have room for additions, changes, alternatives. Revising single-spaced material is nearly impossible.
- Don't be concerned with grammar or spelling errors in your rough draft. Your aim is to get information down—to find out what you have said and what you need to say further. Worrying about errors at this stage will dry up your flow of ideas and associations and tempt you to concentrate on *how* you are saying something rather than on the more important *what.* The result will be, "I may not be saying much, but look how correctly I am saying it!" Correctness *must* come, but it comes *last.* An encouragement: As you work through several drafts, you will be aware that the effort to say something accurately is self-correcting, and your gross mechanical errors will decrease. Here is an interesting footnote: The root meaning (Middle English) of the word *error* suggests

"wandering around looking for something." Think about that. It has been said that "errors are the portals to discovery."

- Be suspicious of generalizations. By themselves, they are either vague or meaningless. More often than not, beginning writers don't know a generalization when they commit one. For example, when you find yourself writing "I like the freedom of being on my own," your internal Reader should snap to attention and ask, "What kind of freedom? Freedom *from* something? From what? Freedom to *do* something? Give an example. 'On your own' in what sense? Financial? Without close supervision?" And so on.

A generalization, like an opinion, has little merit unless it is supported, or led up to, by concrete facts or specific illustrations. The common assertion that "every person has a right to his opinion" is simple nonsense. We have a "right" to voice whatever we wish, but no opinion is worth much unless it is buttressed by evidence. Without evidence, such an opinion is merely a prejudice. Any person has a right to a prejudice, but we don't have to listen to it. Twenty-four hundred years ago, Aristotle, the Greek philosopher-teacher, said, "The speaker, to be believed, must have witnesses and documents and the authority of his own experience."

- Be reckless with your early drafts. Play with words, phrases, the word order within a sentence. Give yourself choices; revision is largely choices.
- Make fullest use of the vocabulary you now have. You have had experience with language since you were a small child. Your useful vocabulary comes from your experience, your work, your leisure, your living. *Don't* use a thesaurus (a dictionary of synonyms); it will tempt you to substitute words for thought. A thesaurus can be useful later, when you have firm control of your prose.
- There are, of course, many times when you must write without time to revise in detail, and I will have more to say about that later. But you can begin to establish the habit of mind which will allow you to revise as you go. That's not easy. But no one has said that good writing is easy.
- Many students have found it useful to use the split-page device, as I did in this chapter, as a self-teaching tool. Line a page vertically down the middle. On the right, copy your draft, double- or triple-spaced. On the left, talk to yourself: Question, criticize, make notes, additions, changes. Try to bring your own internal Reader/Editor alive. You may be surprised at how useful this can be to your own sense of "building" a piece of writing.

REVISING AND EDITING

For my own purposes as I write, I make a clear distinction between revising and editing. You may find this useful, too. Revision is still exploratory: There are often large changes, cuts, additions, and rearrangements. The piece of writing, whatever its length, is structurally unfinished, and some of its elements need redesigning and rebuilding. At this point, the process is still fluid, sloppy. Editing, on the other hand, is more technical, even mechanical: correcting misspellings, grammar, punctuation; weighing one word choice against another; tinkering with sentence rhythms and phrase placements—in a word, *polishing.*

I have found this distinction useful because, despite years of experience, I tend to edit as I go, even in an early draft, and find myself delayed or even stopped by "mistakes" that a part of me wants to correct *now.* This is a kind of obsession, ingrained by early schooling. Beginning writers are especially, and needlessly, tormented by it. The problem is that editing (correcting) gets in the way of production, when it should be the other way around: Editing should come *after* production is largely accomplished. As one writer said pointedly, "The habit of compulsive premature editing doesn't just make writing hard, it also makes writing dead."

Proofreader's Marks

Proofreader's marks are small, useful tools. Use them when you revise your own copy. The marks are standard all over the world, so it pays to know them. The ones most used with manuscripts are shown on page 27. Others, which you can find in any good dictionary, are used to correct words already set in type.

Symbol in Margin	Mark on Copy	Meaning
¶	¶	Start a new paragraph.
ℐ	ℐ	Delete, take ^yᶂout.
∧	∧	Insert indicated word _∧words. *(or)*
(cap)	≡	Make capital letter(s).
(lc)	/	Make lowercase (small letters).
(tr)	∼	Transpose. (Use right the word order.)
(close up)	⌒	Close up space.
(stet)	....	Restore it. (I made a mistake.)
⊙	⊙	Period.
⌃, /	⌃,	Comma at point of insertion.
:	:	Colon. (Remember: Get it right.)
⌃;	⌃;	Semicolon. (Never fear; help is here.)
⌄'	⌄'	Apostrophe. (Williams football.)
⌄''	⌄''	Quotation marks.
=	=	Hyphen. (Two-year, four-year.)

chapter 5

Titles, Leads, and Signposts

Anyone who writes often has difficulty getting started. The blank piece of paper seems to stare at you, daring you to mark it. However, if you have an idea and some information about what you want to say but don't know how to begin, it helps to experiment with titles and leads. You may scrap a title or lead later—you probably will—but your problem is to get moving. A title or a lead will help you *focus* your subject. One immediate caution: Flashy or tricky titles or leads will nearly always get you into trouble. *You must play fair with a reader.* Don't lead the reader to expect what you can't deliver in the rest of the piece. For example:

Title: ANNIHILATION UNLIMITED

Fragment of lead sentence: "An airburst of a 50-megaton hydrogen bomb at 10,000 feet over Washington, D.C., would . . . ." A reader expects a factual, objective development of the cataclysmic effects of an atomic attack: the initial shock wave, the thermal pulse followed by a firestorm, the lethal radiation, and so on.

Title: TEN EASY SUMMER DINNERS

Fragment of lead sentence: "In summer, when you would rather spend every possible minute outdoors, easy-to-get dinners are . . . ." A reader should get both recipes and how-to advice.

Title: ADAPTING YOUR CAR'S CARBURETOR TO ALCOHOL FUEL

Fragment of lead sentence: "Most do-it-yourself mechanics can manage the simple carburetor adjustments . . . ." The reader needs clear, step-by-step description, with simple illustrations or diagrams, showing how to adapt a carburetor to alcohol.

In these examples, leads and titles work together, one supplementing the other. *Lead* is a journalist's term meaning simply "opener," whether it is a sentence or several short paragraphs. It is much to be preferred to *topic sentence* or *thesis statement,* since these two terms almost assume a standard, or acceptable, beginning. The writer should not be straitjacketed by formula limitations.

The lead has several functions:

1. To introduce the subject by telling what the writer is going to say or to introduce a situation that the writer will develop. It is a way to focus and limit a subject.
2. To indicate the direction the writer intends to take: persuasion, how-to, argument, whatever.
3. To lure or attract the reader: to gain initial interest.
4. To suggest the tempo of the writing (how it will move along) and the tone (the writer's attitude, stance, or bias).

There are a dozen or more standard leads. They are seldom found in their pure form, and a combination may produce the best results. Here are eleven leads, listed in approximate order of frequency of use in large, general-circulation magazines.

1. ANECDOTE

An anecdote is a brief story, usually with a point. This lead is especially adaptable to personality sketches or to accounts of personal experience. Here is an example designed to open an article about the professional qualities of a particular teacher.*

We were an awful class. We had terrorized every teacher since the third grade, especially substitutes who would leave at the end of a day shaking, and often in tears. Now we were in seventh grade, veering into puberty,

*Freely adapted from a story by Teresa Foley, "A Lesson in Discipline," *Harper's,* December 1956. Copyright © Teresa Foley. Used by permission.

and just hitting our stride. We were referred to by certain members of the P.T.A. as "Les Misérables."

Seventh grade—and Miss Wiggins. She was new to the school and to us. She was about 40, tall, erect, with a handsome face. She greeted us with a bucket of cold water: No pleas for adjustment, no homilies on the joys of learning. In an even, firm tone she said, "My name is Miss Wiggins. We will be together for a year. I will teach. You will learn. You have thirty seconds to get out lined paper and a pencil, and you will write ten sentences about something you saw on the way to school this morning." It was the shock treatment all right. We scrabbled for paper, pencils.

Then a loud voice from the back of the room: "Crap!" We knew who it was: Billy Jenkins, held back for two years, already bearded and tough, with a voice cracking to bass. He was our "leader." We waited for Miss Wiggins to stammer or cower or temporize, the way the others had done. She simply stared at Billy—for a long time. Then she said, in a quiet tone with steel in it, "Stand up, Billy." It was a simple, inescapable request. He stood. He stood for the rest of the day. Miss Wiggins kept him after school for an hour every day for five months. He never spoke out of turn in class again.

One day, Janie, a classmate who had been helping in the office when the intercom was open to Miss Wiggins's room, said, "She's teachin' him to *read*." When we thought about it, none of us had heard Billy read in class, except for surly mumbles. No teacher had dared call on him.

No wonder Billy couldn't fight her. She was teaching him in private the one thing he needed to give up pretending and fighting back.

2. STARTLING STATEMENT

This is designed to rouse the reader by grabbing attention with an arresting statement. Be careful of this one: You have to *prove* your statement to your reader. Here is a lead by a doctor who takes a position on what to tell terminally ill patients.

> To speak of telling the truth, the whole truth, and nothing but the truth to a terminally ill patient is absurd. It is absurd because it is impossible.

3. NARRATIVE

This differs from the anecdote in that it does not usually have a climax or a point. It's like "Once upon a time . . . and then . . . and then . . . ."

Narrative often takes off with an opening "hook," or arresting statement.

4. SUMMARY

A few sentences or a short paragraph summarizes what the rest of the writing develops in detail.

> The last forty years have possibly been the most extraordinary in human-ity's intellectual history.
>
> Consider. We have discovered continental drift; unlocked the genetic code; recognized the role of toolmaking in our biological evolution; achieved microminiaturization, and thus the microcomputer; invented the laser; undertaken the massive application of solid-state electronics; discov-ered the nerve circuitry that organizes perceptions; penetrated the struc-ture of fundamental particles; possibly identified antimatter; and taken a glimpse of the origin of the universe.

This could be the lead of an article summarizing scientific advances in the last four decades.

5. QUOTATION

An appropriate quotation is often a useful starter. If you use more than one, be sure that they are brief and closely linked. Here is an example of a lead for an article on tips to clear writing:

> "As for style of writing, if one has anything to say, it drops from him simply and directly, as a stone falls to the ground. There are no two ways about it, but down it comes, and he may stick in the points and stops wherever he can get a chance."
>
> Henry David Thoreau was a good example of his own advice. . .

6. QUESTION

One or more questions that lead naturally into the body of the writing make a good lead. Like the striking statement, questions can often be provocative. Here is an example from an article discussing energy dilem-mas:

Is the frequently proclaimed shortage of energy real or contrived? Is nuclear power dangerous, or are the dangers imagined? Is solar energy a valid alternative, or is it only a beguiling possibility?

The questions begin an extended article developed from key words in the lead: *real, contrived, dangerous, imagined, alternative, possibility.*

7. DESCRIPTION

The saying "I'll draw you a picture" has sense when applied to some leads. Sharply focused description—of a situation, place, or person—can get the reader off to a good start. This lead should be tight and brief, with specific images or facts. Here is one for an article on gifted children.

He sits in a highchair in a fuzzy blue sleeper. His fat little fist clutches a pencil, point down. The tip of his tongue sticks out of the corner of his mouth. Slowly, awkwardly, he makes marks on a sheet of paper. The marks are large, sprawling printing. He is making letters, words, and *full sentences.* He is barely three years old.

8. GENERAL STATEMENT

This should leave no doubt in the reader's mind about what is coming:

The brewing of strong drink is as old as man himself. . . .

Or:

"If you make a person think he is thinking, he will love you; but if you *make* him think, he will hate you." (Don Marquis)

9. ANALOGY

An analogy draws a resemblance between things that are otherwise unlike. It is often expressed as an image or a comparison. For example:

A French traveler, early in the nineteenth century, said that "American society is like a glass of beer: foam on top, dregs on the bottom, and clear, settled brew in the middle."

10. STATEMENT OF PURPOSE

The statement of purpose is usually used for how-to articles or for information that you want your reader to have quickly and succinctly. Simply begin by saying flatly what you are going to write about.

> There are some special techniques every nurse needs to know about caring for heavily sedated patients. Here, from my experience, are some of the most important. . . .

11. NEWS LEAD

This is found in any straight news story or publicity release: *who, what, when, where,* and *how* (if known). Leads are usually rewritten several times, often when you have "finished" a piece. But to get you started, invent several titles and leads, and pick the one closest to your intentions.

SUGGESTIONS

- Let me encourage you to experiment with titles and leads. They help you to sharpen your intentions, and they most certainly help with the later organization of whatever you write. (I fussed around with nearly sixty titles for this book until my editor and I agreed on the most appropriate. One rule of thumb is that titles should rarely have more than five words, and subtitles, if any, should be equally brief. Titles should be honest; they should clearly indicate what is going to be delivered.)
- Let me remind you once again—and I will do so many times—that you are learning a *process;* you are not following a cookbook. You are learning how to put into words your own unique (which means one-of-a-kind) vision of one slice of the world.

BUT: There's a bonus, as there always is with honest effort. You will begin to feel—and I assure you of this—that you are learning how to *make* a good piece of work, one that *belongs* to you and to no one else and one that is a clear reflection of yourself to others.

chapter 6

Sentences and Grammar: Muscle and Bones

A sentence is the smallest unit of meaning in our language. The simplest definition of a sentence is that it is a statement that makes sense by itself, without reference to what comes before or after it.

As you rework a draft, you find yourself rewriting the sentences, so you have to consider *grammar* and *syntax*. These terms are almost interchangeable, differing mainly in emphasis. Grammar deals generally with the relations among words and with their functions inside a sentence. Syntax refers to the arrangement of words, phrases, and sentences according to established usage.

Grammar is to language what the skeleton is to a body: the bones, the basic structure. Without a skeleton, a body would be merely a mass of tissue. Without grammar, language too would be shapeless, unable to express thinking adequately. But *the thinking comes first.*

English is a cause-and-effect language, a noun-verb language. It is not an inflected language (in which word meanings are changed by sound or voice pitch). Our sentences have a *subject* (thing or person) *doing* something (verb or predicate) or being done to. (There *are* some subtle inflections, but I won't go into them.)

The business of "grammatical error" is so thorny and worrisome that it actually keeps some people from learning to write. Grammar errors worry teachers, students, employers, and the general public more than anything else about writing except bad spelling. We hear outraged cries or "back to basics" and "drill it into the kids until they never forget it." But most English teachers, when they think about it (which is not often enough), will agree that ninety percent of the time about the same half dozen errors are being committed. Correcting them requires only common sense because *the rules of grammar are based on simple common sense.* Like any good tool, grammar is an aid—in this case an aid to thinking. An ungrammatical sentence is invariably a fuzzy sentence because the thought behind it is fuzzy.

When you write to be understood, you *must* pay attention. Perhaps half the grammatical errors that people commit stem from carelessness or lack of attention. But any person who has passed the written portion of a driver's test can learn to recognize and avoid grammatical errors. You must learn to write grammatically. But you learn best and most surely in the context of your own writing, *as it is going on.* Learning in context is always more effective than learning in bits and pieces. For example, when I used to take people into the wilderness on long canoe trips, I liked teaching them a woodsman's skills so that they could cope, be comfortable, and enjoy their experience. The chief tool of a woodsman is an ax; with it, a skilled person can make almost anything he or she is likely to need. But suppose I had given my greenhorns a typical school situation. Suppose I had handed them a small textbook titled *Care and Use of the Ax*, with chapters on the nomenclature of the ax, felling a tree (with diagrams), cutting a billet (with diagrams), splitting firewood (with diagrams), and so on. After studying each chapter, the "student" would get a quiz. Suppose he made one hundred percent on every quiz. *He has still not yet touched a real ax, and chances are the first time he gets an honest-to-God ax in his hands, he'll split his instep.*

In learning a skill, there is no substitute for hands-on experience. This analogy will serve for grammar, too. Try to say something; *get your hands on it,* and make your corrections either as you go or later as you revise.

THE "RULES"

Some years ago, the Minnesota Newspaper Association published some tongue-in-cheek "backward" rules for reporters that themselves illustrated many common errors. I'll comment briefly about each.

1. *Make each pronoun agree with their antecedent.* This error comes mostly from sloppy speech habits. *Each* is singular (one), and *their* is plural (more than one). If they don't agree, the reader will be confused. The linking of the single (one) to the plural (several) is inexact thinking.
2. *Join clauses good, like a conjunction should.* *Like* is a comparison (meaning "similar to"). It should be *as*, which implies "to the same degree." And *good* should be *well* (as in *well joined*).
3. *About those sentence fragments.* *What* about the fragments? A sentence must make sense by itself. This fragment doesn't.
4. *When dangling, watch your participles.* Don't mistake -*ing* words for verbs unless they are hitched to *are, will, be,* and the like. Then they become verbals, or verb phrases. If you are not sure of -*ing* words, just omit them for a while. Your prose will be stronger. Would you say, "I saw the World Trade Center walking down the street"? That would be some sight.

NOTE: It is permissible to use a sentence fragment for emphasis, even a fragment beginning with an -*ing* word—*provided you know exactly what you are doing.* There are a number of fragments in this book: They are deliberate.

5. *Verbs has to agree with their subject.* Either "A verb (one) *has* to agree with *its* (one) subject" or "Verbs (plural) *have* to agree with *their* (plural) subjects." Pronouns, too, have to agree with subjects. A common error is "Each person should do their thing." *Each* is one; *their* is more than one.
6. *The run-on sentence confuses the reader does not know where to stop.* A run-on, or comma splice, is two full sentences on either side of a comma or two independent clauses (sentences) run together without a stop. The solution is simple: Separate these either by a full stop (period) or by a semicolon, colon, or dash.
7. *Just between you and I, watch the objects of prepositions.* Common prepositions are *for, to, from, by, between, toward, in, into,* and the like. They take an object. Your ear needs to be trained for these.

Would you say, "I bought shoes for she and I"? You would not say "for she" or "for I," would you? Incidentally, it is all right to end a sentence with a preposition if it helps clarify the meaning or if rearranging the sentence would make it sound awkward or unnatural.

8. ***Don't use no double negative.*** Would you say, "She was not the one who didn't run the race"? Takes a while to sort that out. Bad grammar confuses a reader, and a careful writer doesn't do that.

9. ***Try to not split infinitives.*** An infinitive is *to* plus a verb. Cutting the *to* away from the verb is awkward and sometimes misleading. It should be "Try not to split infinitives." It's clearer that way.

PARTS OF SPEECH

We identify parts of speech by the jobs they do in a sentence.

Nouns and **pronouns** *name*. Nothing else names.
Verbs *state*. Nothing else states.
Adjectives and **adverbs** *modify* or *describe*. Nothing else modifies.
Prepositions and **conjunctions** *join* or *place*. Nothing else joins.

EXAMPLE

Prepositions are basically *position* words:

for	from	about	above	below	around	by
with	in	for	up	on	than	of
into	over	beyond	down	within	without	inside
to	beside	through	at	as		

TRY IT BY EAR

Here are some techniques to help you sharpen your ear for sensible (thus "correct") grammar or syntax.

When in doubt, write short, simple, noun-verb sentences. These may sound choppy, but your first obligation is to be clear. If you write

> I have a cat which is a male he weighs over 20 pounds and they are the ones that roam alot and gets into garbage cans at night and he has a big white spot like a diamond on his chest . . . .

STOP. Your *thinking* is not in order. Try this:

I have a male cat. He weighs over 20 pounds. He has a big white spot, like a diamond, on his chest. Male cats roam a lot at night. They get into garbage cans.

That may not be smooth prose, but it is clear. And grammatical.

INDEFINITE REFERENCE

Faulty reference has to do with such pronouns as *this, that, it, the,* and *those.* These are "pointing" words. They say *this* chair, *that* window, *those* baskets. For example, if you begin a piece by saying, "*This* night was one that I will never forget," not only do you point to a night that has not yet been mentioned, but you pile a cliché after it, "I will never forget." Why not say, "Last fall I had a night that terrified me." "Last fall" is more specific than "this," and "that terrified me" suggests that you're not likely to forget it.

Don't be afraid of grammar. Many students say, despairingly, "Oh, I've never been any good at grammar." Saying this, they cut themselves off from learning some simple solutions to grammar problems. *Clarity* is the first, the last, and almost the only objective. When you are thinking clearly, your grammar is more than likely in order. The real question is, *"Am I making sense to my reader?"* It is the *order of thinking* that fixes the grammar—not following rules without understanding them.

MANIPULATING SENTENCES

I discussed technicalities first because they are the most troublesome matters for students and teachers. But a sentence is far more than a technical correctness. It is a writer's delight—and terror. It is a carver's careful tool, a fencer's blade. It is muscle and bones. And before I get hypnotized by metaphor, I'd better turn practical again.

You need to free yourself to manipulate language. Many beginning writers, having put words on paper, assume that what they have said *is* said, as though the sentences were set in concrete. *No way,* as current slang has it. Eventually, sentences have to reflect what you mean as exactly as possible. They have to be molded, tinkered with, rearranged.

There are several ways to reshape sentences. These changes always depend precisely on *what* you mean, not just generally what you think you mean.

PLACEMENT AND RECOMBINING

A good sentence should move cleanly and end in strength, but often, trailing clauses or phrases let the sentence slip away into a mumble. Remind yourself that a sentence is meant to carry only one idea, though the idea may have several parts in clauses, phrases, or single words. The *placement* of these parts qualifies, or even changes, the sentence's meaning. Here is a silly sentence to demonstrate what I mean:

Only I hit him in the eye yesterday.

If you move the word *only* to each position in the sentence, you'll see how the placement alters both meaning and emphasis.

If you get tangled in a long sentence, list its separate elements as statements and then recombine them. Or make separate sentences. You have to ask what the sentence is building toward, and your *ear* can help you with the rhythm of it. Here's an example of an awkward sentence:

Lonely, bitter, and disillusioned, Beth shuffled into the bus station, her shoulders bowed and her suitcase heavy in her hand.

The sentence is too full. I asked the student to break it into separate statements, since there are, in fact, several potential sentences within this awkward one. She wrote:

Beth was lonely.
Beth was disillusioned.
Beth was bitter.
She shuffled into the bus station.
Her shoulders were bowed.
Her suitcase hung heavy in her hand.

I asked the student what she felt was the important part of the statement. She said, "Her bitterness." I suggested that she end the sequence of ideas with this. Her first version:

Beth's suitcase hung heavy in her hand. Shoulders bowed, she shuffled into the bus station. She was bitter, disillusioned, and lonely.

Her second version:

> Beth shuffled into the bus station, her suitcase heavy in her hand. Her
> shoulders were bowed. She was bitter, disillusioned, and lonely.

Either of these versions is better than the first one. But the point is that
in manipulating these sentences, the student came to understand that *she*
could control meaning and emphasis in what she was saying.

SUBORDINATION

Often, subordination at the end of a sentence weakens it.

> Major factors in weather patterns are jet streams, which are substrato-
> spheric.

An improvement would be to tie *substratospheric* to *jet stream* or to
change the sentence's structure further.

> Substratospheric jet streams are major factors in weather patterns.

Even better would be

> Jet streams—fast-moving substratospheric winds—are major factors in
> weather patterns.

CADENCE OR RHYTHM

The movement of sentences can reflect their meaning. The best illustration may be in excerpts from letters I've had from writer friends about
two different experiences.

EXAMPLE 1

The writer had been through a terrifying hurricane. Events happened to
him suddenly, without warning. Notice how abrupt the sentences are.
They reflect the successive shocks of the experience. Then look at the
verbs: *roared, screamed, banged, shuddered, exploded, slammed, slid,*

crawled, yanked, and the adverb *violently.* This may be overwritten, but it was a personal letter, and we seldom revise letters.

> Worst were the big gusts. The steady wind simply roared. But with a gust, it screamed, and a loose shutter banged and banged and banged against the clapboards. The house shuddered—moved. Rain hit the windows like steel pellets. I couldn't see out the bedroom window, and I turned away. Then the window exploded. The back of my neck felt hot knife points of glass. The gust slammed me against the wall. The heavy bed slid toward me. I crawled to the door. I couldn't open it against the wind. When the gust dropped, I yanked it open. On hands and knees, I crawled toward the stairs. The door swung violently shut behind me.

The writing, almost jerky, reflects the reality.

EXAMPLE 2

The writer lives by the rocky Maine seacoast. He said, just before the passage below, "I think of Jon on his little dragger in those inexorable seas—men who go down to the sea in ships, such small ships, in such an immensity."

> It was lovely by the shore tonight. The moon was full, and there was a soft on-shore breeze. But there must have been a storm far out to sea. The swells were as high as I have seen them for a long time. They sucked back from the tidal pools, rearing higher and higher, and then, curling into crests, surged toward shore, to slam down on the ledges with a thud I could feel under my feet, creaming into crevices, throwing spume that I could taste salty on my lips, then rushing back to melt into another surge, heaving up, silver and white-crested in the moonlight, to assault again.

Begin the sentence "They sucked back from the tidal pools . . ." and read it aloud, slowly, pausing at the commas. The sentence surges, as the sea does, in the rhythm the writer wants to communicate.

CAUTION: Be careful not to make your sentence rhythms contrived or artificial; they *must* correspond to reality. Again, note the verbs and verbals: *sucked, slam, throwing, creaming, rushing back, heaving up, to assault.* This is a risky use of *-ing* words, but it works. Use the technique with care, as you would any sharp instrument.

DICTIONARIES

Own one. A good one. No matter what kind of work you do after you finish your schooling, you will find that a dictionary (a surprisingly modest investment) is a tool you will need and use in all sorts of circumstances.

Don't settle for a paperback. Most of these, even though they may say "Webster" in the title, have less than 10,000 terms, defined skimpily—not enough for a language that has over 900,000 terms. For regular use, get a "collegiate" dictionary (there are four or five good ones) that has 150,000 terms or more. Such dictionaries also usually have brief, authoritative essays on word usage, lexicography (word sources, pronunciation customs, and the like), the making of bibliographies, grammar and syntax, and general rules of spelling. If you intend to go into a career where words and their usages are especially important (law, business, teaching), Webster's hefty *Unabridged Third New International Dictionary* is an investment you will be glad you made.

Don't study your dictionary; play with it. Look up odd or interesting words. Figure out the roots of words; your dictionary will tell you how to do this. Learn to distinguish current from obsolete meanings, or "standard" from local or colloquial ones. Such "playing" is an almost guaranteed way to increase your useful vocabulary. A good dictionary is much like a rich mine, crammed with nuggets of information, quotations, even insights.

MORE ABOUT WORDS

Words are the particles of writing, the bits of mosaic to be fitted together. Or they can be thought of as the separate notes in a musical phrase. Words have *denotation* (meaning or definition) and *connotation* (suggestion, overtones). They have sound, color, rhythm. Many words can mean close to the same thing; others can sound alike but mean different things. They can be slippery, stubborn, and elusive, or clear, helpful, and stimulating. English is a marvelously rich, supple language, capable of easily expressing an incredible range of thoughts, activities, feelings, and insights. Perhaps it is this very richness that tempts us to slipshod use or to choose words carelessly because they "sound" right. Semanticists, who study meaning, remind us that "the word is not the thing," not the reality, just as "the map is not the territory," not the actual ground. These are good mottoes for a writer.

I have suggested that you play with language, manipulate it, make mistakes with it. I recommend, too, that occasionally you have fun with it. I have worked with many a beginning writer who broke loose into confidence by fiddling around: writing limericks, tongue-in-cheek descriptions, wild anecdotes about experiences. The resulting writing usually wasn't much good, but the writers' awareness that they could at least begin to make language do their bidding was exhilarating.

Here are two "reverse examples." I call them this because sometimes we can learn much from the opposite of a proper prescription. (I have never felt that learning should be grimly serious—as perhaps you've gathered.)

First is a descriptive paragraph written by Mark Twain, one of America's finest writers. Read it carefully. Is it good description? Fair? Poor? Before reading further in the chapter, jot down your judgment—what you like or don't like.

It was a crisp and spicy New England morning in early October. The lilacs and laburnums, lit with the glory fires of autumn, hung burning and flashing in the brilliant air, a fairy bridge provided by kind Nature for the wingless wild things that have their homes in the treetops and would visit together. The larch and the pomegranate flung their purple and yellow flames in broad splashes along the slanting westward sweep of the woodland; and the sensuous fragrance of innumerable deciduous flowers rose upon the atmosphere in a swoon of incense. Far in the empty sky, a solitary pharynx slept among the empyrean on motionless wing. And everywhere brooded stillness, serenity, and the peace of God.

After you have noted your reactions, look at the following comments.

Although it sounds like fine writing, the paragraph is deliberate nonsense. Mark Twain wrote it for a young, pretentious would-be writer to show that what may sound impressive or "artistic" can be meaningless. The paragraph is a spoof and a hoax. If you were taken in—even a little—you'd better think harder about words.

Lilacs: bloom only in early spring; in fall, the bushes are dusky green.
Laburnum: a Eurasian variety of poisonous shrub, not found in the North Temperate Zone of the United States.
Wingless wild things: monkeys? squirrels? ostriches? a "bridge" hanging over plants?
Larch: has short, pinelike leaves in bunches, generally a bluish green.

Pomegranates: usually found in hot, arid regions of the Middle East; leaves are bright green, with orange-red flowers and red berries. "Purple and yellow"?

Fling a flame: How? left-handed? in splashes? How do you fling a flame that splashes?

Deciduous flowers: all flowers are deciduous.

Swoon: a fainting fit or attack.

Pharynx: the part of the alimentary canal between the mouth cavity and the esophagus. What's it doing in the sky?

Brood: to dwell continuously and moodily on something. Does serenity brood? Does stillness? And if the "peace of God" broods, then I will choose the Other Place, where I hear there is a Hell of a lot going on.

Note the actual meaning of some of these words; then reread the paragraph to appreciate the humor better—and to appreciate Twain's skill, too.

Again in the spirit of fun, here is something a friend sent me years ago. He doesn't know the source (there was probably more than one), and I don't either, so I can't give a proper attribution. My friend works in one of Washington's large bureaucracies, and a bureaucratic specialty is murdering language by obfuscation. (Now *there's* a word. It means "to confuse, to cover up by masking.") The gadget shown here is a Buzzphrase Generator—it effortlessly produces meaningless bureaucratic jargon. You can use it to give you what sounds like instant expertise on any subject, whether you are familiar with it or not. The Generator has three columns of words numbered from 0 to 9.

0. integrated	0. management	0. options
1. total	1. organization	1. flexibility
2. systematized	2. monitored	2. capability
3. parallel	3. reciprocal	3. mobility
4. functional	4. digital	4. programming (program)
5. responsive	5. modular	5. concept(s)
6. optimal	6. transitional	6. time frame
7. synchronized	7. incremental	7. projection
8. compatible	8. third-generation	8. hardware (software)
9. balanced	9. state-of-the-art	9. contingency

Using the Generator is easy. When you want to insert an "authoritative" phrase, select any three-digit number at random and take the corresponding buzzword from each column. For example, 257: number 2 from the first column, number 5 from the second column, and number 7 from the third. Result: *systemized modular projection.* You don't know what it means. Don't worry; neither will anyone else. But they won't dare question you, because it sounds as though you knew something.

This is not language; it is incantation—a witch doctor stomping around a fire, throwing newt's eyes, frog's toes, and magic powders into a kettle. *We are surrounded by this stuff.* If you don't believe me, read the course descriptions in most college or university catalogs. (Many of these belong on the fiction shelf of a library.) Or if you want a sobering dash, just try to translate the instructions in your annual tax form. One way to beat this insidious game is to learn language solidly enough (*a*) to learn when you are being had and (*b*) to fight back.

If you're feeling wicked, you might sneak a couple of Buzzword phrases into a paper or report and see what happens. You will have mastered number 565, and you will be an example of number 431.

This Generator was typed on number 248, following number 915, for the purpose of giving you number 070. Translation: I typed the Generator on a typewriter, in an orderly way, to give you some choices.

SUGGESTIONS

- Try, deliberately, to write a descriptive piece like Twain's. Make lavish use of adjectives and adverbs. (Describe a specific place or have a specific circumstance in mind.) Be flowery, wordy—and inexact, if you wish. *Then edit what you have written* to squeeze out all unnecessary words or phrases. I have seen many beginning writers gain a surer understanding of words by trying this.
- Write a report or a memo using several phrases from the Buzzword Generator. *Then translate these phrases* into specific meaning, as I did in the last sentence before "Suggestions."

The purpose here is simple: You need to become aware of the weakness and essentially meaningless quality of elaborate and artificial phrasing.

chapter *7*

Punctuation

There are not many precise rules, despite grammar manuals, for commas, semicolons, and the other typographical marks we use to indicate pauses in written speech. We have only a few stops (places for a reader to pause or take note): period, semicolon, colon, dash, question mark, and parentheses. (An editor once said, "Forget the exclamation point. It should be used only for swearing or direct commands. Otherwise, it reminds me of a kid jumping around the page on a pogo stick. Makes me nervous.")

These few punctuation marks are remarkably easy to understand, if you strip away the finicky rules that have grown up around them.

Punctuation marks are signals to readers. They tell them when to pause, when to stop, when a question has been asked. Except for direct quotations, or quotes within quotes, there are two simple ways to think about these marks.

1. Think of punctuation as breathing or pausing:

Comma	**,**	Half a breath.
Semicolon	**;**	Three-quarters of a breath.
Period	**.**	A full breath.
Colon	**:**	"Stop, a list is coming."
Dash	**—**	"Emphasis, side comment, definition coming."
Parentheses	**( )**	"I want to tuck a quick fact or comment here."

2. Or think of punctuation as traffic signals:

Comma	**,**	Flashing yellow light: Slow down; look right and left.
Semicolon	**;**	Flashing red light: Come almost to a stop; then go.
Period	**•**	Stop sign: Stop full, then go.
Colon	**:**	Arrow or road sign: "Food, Fuel, Lodging, Next Right."
Dash	**—**	Detour—be alert.
Parentheses	**( )**	"Caution, alternate route."

If you wonder how to punctuate a sentence, read it aloud. Where are the natural pauses? How long do you want your reader to breathe, to pause? Learn to read your own writing aloud to yourself, slowly, sentence by sentence.

ONE SIMPLE RULE: You may put a full sentence (independent clause) on either side of a semicolon, a colon, a period, or a dash, or within parentheses—but *not* on either side of a comma, unless you have a compound sentence with a conjunction such as *and* or *but*. The comma splice, or comma fault, places a comma where we need a period (usually) or a semicolon. It "splices" (fastens together) two complete sentences. Example: The car swerved off the road, it went into a ditch.

MOST COMMON AND ANNOYING ERROR

The most persistent mechanical error is a punctuation mistake as in "The elephant lifted *it's* trunk." *STOP!* One of the easiest rules to remember is: *The total number of possessive pronouns that have an apostrophe is one: one's.* So it's always *ours, yours, hers, theirs, its, whose, oneself.*

PERSONAL FAVORITE

I like the semicolon as the most flexible of punctuation marks. (It's a journalist's favorite, too.) It can separate independent clauses (full sentences); it can serve as a longer stop than a comma in a series of phrases where you want separate emphasis; or it can either link or contrast logically connected elements within a sentence—as in this one. But be careful not to overuse it. On an early draft of this book, my editor said, "You scatter semicolons with wild abandon." He was right.

chapter 8

Paragraphs

A paragraph is hard to define; even the dictionary is evasive about it. The dictionary is, however, certain about typography: The first line of a paragraph is usually indented (brought to the right several spaces) from the left-hand margin.

The Greeks indicated a kind of paragraph break with a mark or short line (*graphos*) in the margin beside (*para*) lines of writing. There is speculation that the modern indented paragraph was invented by newspapers, which needed to have chunks of coherent meaning so that a story could be chopped off to fit column lengths and still convey the basic information. Current usage, as in business letters, frequently features *un*indented paragraphs, separated by double spacing.

A paragraph can consist of one to several dozen sentences, depending on its function. The dictionary says that a paragraph "forms a new rhetorical unit." That might be helpful, except that *rhetorical* is tough to define too. Practically speaking, a paragraph can be a brief development of a single idea or statement, or it can be a collection of information that hangs together. When you shift to another idea, or even a different emphasis of the same idea, it's time for a new paragraph. It's much like shifting gears in a stick-shift car. Modern usage prefers short paragraphs because they are easier for a reader.

If we could visualize a paragraph, we'd see four basic formats:

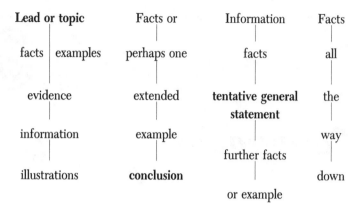

Lead or topic	Facts or	Information	Facts
facts │ examples	perhaps one	facts	all
evidence	extended	**tentative general statement**	the
information	example		way
illustrations	**conclusion**	further facts	down
		or example	

But these schemes can be misleading because they point toward a "formula" for paragraphing. Indeed, most students are taught the formula known as the **T** shape. There are dozens of rhetoric books that describe it at portentous length: topic (or thesis) sentence, development with specific support, conclusion. However, this may not work when you write a piece with many paragraphs. In such a case, you may have paragraphs that are simply collections of information that belong together, without a topic sentence or tidy development.

There are simply no fixed rules for paragraphing. You have to learn to *sense* when you move from one group of related facts to another. As always, it's a matter of thinking clearly and of keeping your reader in mind. While you are learning, if you are in doubt about when to make a paragraph, do it.

You may have noticed how short most of the paragraphs are in this book. That's no accident. I want you to keep reading.

chapter 9

Wordiness

We are often tempted to use empty words or phrases. They "sound better," some people say. But flowery words, usually adjectives or adverbs, should be used like chili or garlic—with care. (Voltaire said that "the adjective is the enemy of the noun.") Some teachers, sad to say, encourage students to use elaborate vocabularies. Such teachers should be stood against a blackboard to write a thousand times: "I will not encourage fancy writing." Then they should have to write a piece for a tough editor.

If English is your native language, chances are you have enough words to make yourself understood clearly. Even a basic vocabulary (1,800 to 2,500 words) will allow you to say what you mean. Most of the language we use each day in ordinary living, where our guts and feelings are, comes from Anglo-Saxon root words, usually of one syllable: *love, hate, pain, hurt, glad, cry, cut, walk, run, bite, kiss.*

If you are afflicted by wordiness, you have a few basic remedies:

STRUCTURAL CHANGES

Avoid the Passive Voice

The passive is the voice of the bureaucrat; it avoids commitment. Instead of "Problems were found by us," say "We found problems." Two words saved. Stronger statement. Once in a rare while, you will need to use the passive because it makes sense in context. But stay away from it as a matter of practice.

Use Direct Verbs

While you are learning to use the language you have with sureness, stay away from -*ing* words. They trap you into thinking they are verbs. They're not: Usually they are participles, half verb and half adjective, and they need helping verbs like *will* or *are*. Instead of "We were talking," say, "We talked."

When possible, avoid "to be" or forms of it. It blunts meaning. Instead of "George is willing to be a volunteer," say, "George will volunteer."

Simplify Sentence Structure

Avoid complicated sentences. Complex sentences (with dependent clauses) or compound sentences (with independent clauses and conjunctions) are just right—sometimes. But if you find yourself stringing out "and . . . and . . . and . . . ," break the sentence into two or even three shorter ones. Too long a collection of relative clauses can bog your reader in a swamp of confusion. Beware especially of *which* clauses. "Whiches," said James Thurber, "multiply like rabbits. One which leads to another, and you end up tweeting like a bird."

VOCABULARY CHANGES

Reduce the Syllable Count

If you are experiencing the malady of polysyllables (this sentence is already wheezing), write a paragraph in words of one syllable. The content of the paragraph is not important, but your effort to write it will be salutary (fancy language for "good for you.") Here is an example:

> We are too rich in words, and hence we tend to waste them. Long words tempt us, since they seem to show that we know more than we do. But short words do not let us hide what we do not know. These are words we use each day to tell us how we feel or what we think. When we love, we want to hug or kiss or say soft things. If we feel joy, we may sing or dance.

If we feel hate, our words are harsh and we may curse. Short words tell what we are: They are strong and say what is real.

Do, of course, use words of more than one syllable where they are necessary, accurate, or appropriate. But *watch* them. Their propensity is to proliferate (multiply, or produce more like themselves) to the point of redundancy.

See?

Avoid Worn-Out Words

When we talk, we often overuse or misuse a few familiar words until they are nearly meaningless. These words are "intensifiers," and when we use them in speech, we add stress or tone of voice or gestures for emphasis. But when the words slop over into writing, they constitute "semantic noise" and contribute only to vagueness. Because the words are abused and tired, cut them out of your written vocabulary for a while. This will force you to search for more accurate or appropriate language to clarify your meaning. Here is a sample list:

	Worn, Misused Meaning	True Meaning
all right	very good	satisfactory
cute	youthfully pretty	shrewd, keen
fabulous	extremely good	unbelievable
fantastic	extremely good	strange, weird, bizarre
great	good, enjoyable	of significant importance or size
plus	and	added to
quite	somewhat, rather	completely, entirely

	Worn, Misused Meaning	True Meaning
really	very	in reality
terrible	bad	invoking terror or dread
terrific	extremely good	fearful, frightful
very	to a high degree	exact, true

There are other words that are misused or tiresomely repeated, but this list should sensitize you a little to boring language, spoken or written. (One current TV commercial for hot dogs use *great* nine times in thirty seconds.) For the fun of it, try mocking or rewriting some commercial slogans or phrases as they beat your ears (and brain) with blah words.

chapter **10**

Limp Language: Clichés

Standard advice is: Avoid clichés. Why? What are clichés? Clichés are trite, hackneyed phrases, tired language made meaningless by thought-less overuse. Once they may have been fresh and even amusing. Now, they are like prefabricated word patterns printed on tape, to be pasted into a sentence when a writer is too lazy or uncaring to find accurate language.

How do you know when you are committing a chiché? Simple. Ask yourself if you know *precisely* what the expression means. Here are five common clichés, with their meanings explained. If you have used one of these, did you know its meaning—or did you write it hoping your reader would know? Or didn't you care?

Dead as a doornail. What is a doornail? It is the pin around which a hinge turns. The pin does not move and is therefore "dead."

Happy as a clam at high tide. At high tide, water covers clam flats, so clams cannot be dug up. Happy un-dug clams.

Incontrovertible fact. By definition, a fact is provable, demonstrable, and thus incontrovertible. The combination is redundant. (Look up the word.)

Method in his madness. A corruption from Shakespeare's *Hamlet.* Po-lonius says, "Though this be madness, yet there is method in't."

Acid test. Do you know the function of litmus papers and certain reagents to test for acids?

Here are more then ten dozen clichés. Writing afflicted with these things will inevitably be flabby, dull, and misleading.

a babe in the woods
a barrel of monkeys
abreast of the times
a bull in a china shop
a day I will never forget
a few well-chosen words
after all is said and done
all in all
all too soon
an impressive sight
any port in a storm
any way, shape, or form
appeared on the scene
as luck would have it
a stitch in time
at long last
at this point in time
be-all and end-all
believe it or not
best-laid plans
bittersweet memories
black as night (pitch)
bloodcurdling scream
blushing bride
bolt from the blue
breakneck speed
budding genius
busy as a bee
butterflies in my stomach
by leaps and bounds
caught like rats in a trap
clear as crystal
cool as a cucumber
crying need

doomed to disappointment
  (failure)
each and every
easier said than done
eats like a hog (pig, horse, bird)
equal to the occasion
far-fetched idea
fat, dumb, and happy
felt need
feverish haste
filled with happiness
fits like a glove
flood of tears
foregone conclusion
fought like a tiger
funny as a crutch
goes without saying
good as gold
great honor (privilege)
green as grass
hard as nails
have the privilege
head over heels
heart in my throat
hectic experience
higher than a kite
hot as hell
if you can't be good, be careful
in the last (final) analysis
in the nick of time
in today's society
last but not least
leave no stone unturned
like a child with a new toy

line of least resistance
long-felt want
long-suffering
loose as a goose
lucky in love
madly in love
make ends meet
meek as a lamb
nestled in the hills
never in the history of
none the worse for wear
nutty as a fruitcake
present day generation
psychological moment
quick (fast) as lightning
really
red-letter day
ripe old age
rooted to the spot
sadder but wiser
safety in numbers
sickening thud

smart as a whip
stiff upper lip
stubborn as a mule
take in stride
the bottom line
throw new light on
tidy sum
time and time again
tired but happy
tired to death
to the bitter end
unheard-of happiness
untold riches
up the creek without a paddle
very much in evidence
viable
we feel bound to point out
wended their way
whatever the case
with bated breath
words fail to express
you know what I mean (y'know)

And surely you know someone who is *crazy as a loon* or who has *bats in his belfry.* Life is full of *endless problems,* and there are *many pitfalls before us.* Do we try and try *to the last gasp?* Is there an *endless vista?* Have you *had it up to here* with problems? Don't despair, *everything will come out all right.*

Everybody's got troubles, buddy. *So what's your problem?*

Is this guy *as phony as a wooden nickel?* Gird up your lions, Mac. *Faint heart never won fair lady. Give 'em an inch, and they'll take a mile.*

You win a few and lose a few. Those are the breaks.

Yeah, *I must've been blind.*

You better believe it.

You see? You can be *carried away* by this stuff. You're seduced into thinking that you are saying something meaningful. You're not; you're just making noise. Clichés are as firm as wet Kleenex.

Everyone speaks clichés from time to time. But writing is not speaking: It must be more deliberate, more exact, more thoughtful. How can you avoid clichés? As a start, become familiar with this list, which, alas, is by no means complete. But I think I have given you enough examples so that you can begin to tune your ear for these insidious expressions.

If a phrase comes too easily, seems too pat, suspect it; ask questions of it. Do I mean to say this? Or is the phrase *tailor-made* (another cliché) and pasted into a sentence to save thinking? I can't emphasize this enough, because clarity is central to communication: *You have to care about your reader.* If you were in his or her place, would you really know what you were talking about?

chapter 11

Search, Find, and Write

Many jobs, in school and out, require you to search for information from various sources, to organize it, and to state it compactly in your own words. This is "research" in a sense, and it's a kind of writing you should learn to do.

Since this is a book about learning how to write, I won't consider here the requirements of a lengthy academic research paper, with its apparatus of footnotes and bibliography. Few people write these after college. You can learn more about writing by doing shorter papers (three to four double-spaced pages) about a severely limited aspect of a subject. Remember that one of your aims is to write *more* about *less*. If you want to explore a subject in depth, write a series of short chapters or sections.

SUGGESTIONS

- Approach the job in steps.
- As in your first prewriting, be as specific as possible and limit your subject as strictly as your present knowledge permits. As you search for information, you will probably see ways to focus even more.

59

1. FIND SOURCES

Try to find at least three or four sources for a short paper.

- Check the subject index of the card catalog in your library for books. Many of these cards have chapter headings.
- Do the same for the *Readers' Guide to Periodical Literature.*
- Scan the indexes in encyclopedias, both general and specialized.
- Interview experts or people who have special knowledge in the area you are researching. They will yield firsthand information and will probably suggest further sources.
- Your own direct experience and observation can, in certain areas, give you much of the information you want. For example, you can do comparison shopping in two or three stores to write up a report. Or a nursing student who has done special research on caring for depressed or aggressive patients can do a brief article on that.

Even in libraries that are not as fully equipped as a big university library, you can often find abundant material in specific book chapters or in magazine and journal articles. Don't get discouraged.

2. GATHER YOUR SOURCES

- Scan your sources quickly. Where you can, jot down notes on substance, not full sentences. Though your sources may be secondary, your own writing should be in *your* words, your own sentence structures. (*Plagiarism:* The copyright law specifies that using more than fifty sequential words of another person's writing, without quoting or giving credit, is stealing. Longer passages require written permission.)
- In your search, you may find something different from what you expected. Let your research guide you to new conclusions.
- Compare conflicting authorities and draw your own conclusions.
- Always keep an eye out for an interesting anecdote or an illuminating example.

When you have enough material (you should have gathered about twice as much as you think you will need), sit down to write.

3. ASK: WHAT DO I WANT TO SAY ABOUT THIS INFORMATION?

- Write half a dozen short leads. These are only drafts, but they will help you establish the direction and organization of your notes. Choose the lead that appears to fit your intentions.
- Organize your notes roughly.

4. BEGIN A ROUGH DRAFT

- Write this draft in chunks or blocks. Don't try to write from beginning to end; that only gets you into what I call a snowplow or bulldozer situation: You shove until you stall, back up, and shove some more. Rather, pick from your notes related material you feel comfortable with, and try to develop that into a web of meaning that hangs together. Do several blocks this way, whatever the length of each, and never mind the order. Don't worry about assembling the blocks—that comes later.
- Write in short paragraphs.
- Here's a working note: Except for a typewriter and a batch of pencils, a professional writer's most useful tools are apt to be a pair of scissors and a roll of Scotch tape. More often than not, writers will do segments or pieces of a complete article and then rearrange these physically in logical order.

5. FEEL FOR A FORM

When you have several blocks, *feel for a form.* Sometimes material will point toward a memorandum, with numbered paragraphs, making a sequence of information. Some material will suggest alternating paragraphs, where the purpose is to compare or contrast, as in the comparison-shopping example suggested earlier. Whatever the form, use typography—the arrangement of copy on a page, numbers, letters, type symbols—in the way best suited to help your reader.

EXAMPLE

The form most used now in general-circulation magazines and journals is the feature article. The feature is flexible. It can range from 500 to 3,000 words—rarely more than that. It differs from a formal paper or research thesis principally in that it is designed to interest a reader, as well as to inform. In schematic form, here is the feature's "shape":

This scheme does not represent any set number of blocks or any number of paragraphs within a block.

This is *not* a formula. It is a way of handling the writing process for development of a subject in some detail.

There may be more blocks or fewer, more development within a single block or less.

```
┌─────────────┐
│    Lead     │
└─────────────┘
        >
┌─────────────┐
│   Block of  │
│   meaning   │
│ that hangs  │
│  together   │
└─────────────┘
        >
┌─────────────┐
│    Block    │
└─────────────┘
        >
┌─────────────┐
│    Block    │
└─────────────┘
        >
┌─────────────┐
│    Block    │
└─────────────┘
        >
┌─────────────┐
│     End     │
└─────────────┘
```

After blocks are arranged in logical order, write transitions (>). These may be one or two sentences or a whole paragraph. They are called "bridges" by journalists, and this is an accurate term. They "bridge" one group of meanings to another.

The "end" is not the traditional summary or "conclusion." Rather, it is often an example or illustration that reflects the body of the article.

When you have assembled your blocks and rough transitions, you have a discovery draft. From now on, you must do revising and editing. You cut. You add. You rewrite paragraphs within the blocks and polish transitions. From this point, give your attention to sentences. Then you will probably rewrite your lead for the seventeenth time.

Here is a portion of a student writer's feature (short) on the northern lights, or *aurora borealis*. The example is not fully quoted because, again,

I want you to focus on the structure of the piece rather than to analyze what someone else has written.

TITLE: Heavenly Curtains

LEAD: In this case, a description.

> One night when I was by a lake in Minnesota, I saw the northern lights. They looked like white spotlights shining up into the darkness. Then they wavered and shimmered and showed some green, red, and pink. They covered a whole arc of sky. They were utterly silent.

Information from research

> This brief block tells about when the aurora borealis usually occurs during the year; average frequency; where most usually seen.

Information from research

> This block—longer—is a scientific explanation: It describes the earth's magnetic field, tells of the excitation of upper-atmosphere electrons by the sun's radiation and of the special effects of so-called sunspots, or bursts of sun energy.

END: Descriptive, to match lead.

> The most dazzling display I ever saw was in late August. The whole northern quadrant of the sky was veiled by these heavenly curtains—white-green-pink-red—moving and pulsing. Somehow, I felt in touch with the universe.

This article was brief, barely 800 words. It began and ended with personal experience, but the two intervening blocks were based on research into the nature and cause of the northern lights.

The writer was not especially expert in "science." Indeed, the article developed from her curiosity about something she had seen, something that had impressed and moved her deeply. *She went looking for information,* then *wrote the article mainly to satisfy her own curiosity.*

I can think of no better reason to write. This student writer, at first, had no particular interest in science. But—and this is crucial—she had an interest in explaining to herself something that had impressed her profoundly.

In part, this is what I mean when I say that writing is exploration and discovery.

chapter 12

Writing Tasks— From Simple to Complex

All writing is functional. It *does* something: transmits information, persuades, interprets, analyzes; evokes feeling or insight, as in a poem; reflects personal responses to experiences; demands (requests) a response, as in a complaint to a business or government organization. The form of the writing is a result of its purpose. As in nature, form follows function, not the other way around.

In school, you are apt to do special kinds of writing: term papers, reports, essays, exams, laboratory or case reports, interpretations of reading. Later, in your personal and working life, you will have to do more writing than you thought you would. Despite the telephone, computers, and other information-transmitting machines, the volume of paper work in organizations increases annually. Somebody writes that stuff. It may well be you. When you are in high school or college, can you predict whether one day you will be publicity chairman of a group? Make public speeches? Design and write brochures, sales materials, procedure manuals?

Once you have developed it, writing facility is transferable; you don't need a special course in a specific kind of writing. But you do need experience in solving various kinds of expression problems.

RHETORICAL MODES

Most of the writing we do in our working lives (including college) is called *exposition*—writing that explains or *exposes* information or ideas. We write course papers, term papers, essay examinations, reports; or memoranda, letters, business or professional summaries, analyses, programs. The raw material of all this exposition is *information*.

There are many ways to handle information. Each depends on the purpose of a piece of writing and the audience for which it is written. Exposition is often subdivided into types or patterns of expression, so-called rhetorical modes. Each of them is simply a way of handling a specific writing problem or function. They are seldom used alone or in their "pure" form. The process of exposition of a single problem often requires sensory detail (description), a sequence of happenings (narration), and perhaps a comparison or an analogy.

The best way to learn these techniques is not in isolation—as separate "forms"—but rather as appropriate responses to a variety of writing requirements. Since you will find the rhetorical modes developed in detail in many composition books, it might be useful if I list them and briefly characterize each one. Just remember that you will nearly always find yourself using a mix of these as you try to express what is on your mind.

1. DESCRIPTION

We rarely write purely descriptive pieces. But description is almost always an element in any exposition, since it is making word pictures of scenes or persons or even ideas to help us explain something. Description can either be personal (impressionistic, subjective) or factual (objective). For example, of a summer day, we can say, "It's oppressively hot" (subjective) or "It's 101 degrees with 95 percent humidity" (objective). The essence of good description is the selection of specific detail.

2. NARRATION

Narration is essentially the telling of facts (real or imaginary) *in sequence.* (There are exceptions to this in fiction, but we're dealing here with exposition.) The emphasis is sequence for explanation. Perhaps the simplest example of this is the relating of the steps in a process, like starting a car or, even simpler, a recipe.

3. CLASSIFICATION

This is an effective way of sorting out facts and information according to a reasonably logical system. It is a kind of outline. The choir director, for instance, may classify voices: soprano, alto, contralto, tenor, baritone, bass. The writer of a social or historical essay may divide the discussion into political, military, and economic categories—and perhaps even subdivide these. Although classifying is an obvious step in solving some writing problems, it does tend to be used more in formal presentations, such as an analysis or a strict summary of material.

4. COMPARISON AND CONTRAST

This is such a natural way of explanation that we begin to use it spontaneously as small children. One thing is *like* another, or the opposite of another, or different from another.

There are two things to remember when you compare or contrast:

- Give your separate items or subjects similar treatment. Separate points made for one should be made for the other, usually in the same order. For example, if you are comparing two kitchen knives, you might call attention to function (design), hardness of steel, resistance to rust, holding of an edge, kind of handle, and so on, for each knife.
- If you compare only two subjects, give the pertinent information for each, then summarize briefly. If the comparison is complex and there are several important points to be made about each subject, a better approach might be to alternate separate points and then make a summary and judgment at the end.

5. ANALOGY

Analogy is a form of comparison, usually with a specific application: to explain a complex matter, or an abstract one, by showing that it is similar to (like) something else that is better known or easier to understand. In an analogy, the comparison is between *two different classes of fact*. For example, Einstein used a moving train and its stationary roadbed in several analogies to illustrate concepts of his relativity theory: the relativity of space, time, speed, distance, and so on. He used the same moving train, speeding *away* and sounding its bell, to explain the Doppler effect of receding sound.

Academic cynics have referred to college curricula as race tracks, where students race around in fixed paths. (The Latin *curriculum* does, in fact, mean "race track.") The analogy highlights some harsh criticism of academic routine and rigidity.

6. DEFINITION

See page 72.

7. PROCESS

Basically, this mode tells how the separate steps of an operation lead to its completion; think of it as the "how to do it" or the "how it works" mode. See page 75.

8. CAUSE AND EFFECT

If process analysis usually explains *how*, cause-and-effect analysis emphasizes *why*. Since the relationship between a specific cause and a particular effect may be complex and unclear, you need to use evidence, supporting testimony, or illustrative examples to show how one thing leads to another. Think of cause and effect as the links in a chain: Each link should be as strong and demonstrable as possible.

CAUTION: When you trace a series of causes, don't take for granted that your reader will automatically supply connections that you leave out or forget. Sequence and connections of causes are the key to believability.

9. INDUCTION AND DEDUCTION

These are thinking processes basic to all exposition. Generally, induction leads *from* particular facts *to* an eventual generalization or inclusive statement, and deduction moves in the opposite direction. Whichever the case, the key to persuasion in such reasoning is strong, verifiable evidence, enough of it either to support a valid general statement or to lead to one.

Comment

I have deliberately refrained from developing this brief discussion of the rhetorical modes because it is a mistake to emphasize the *forms* of exposition. These are *ex post facto* results (results coming after the fact) of coping with varied problems of expression. The modes are academic classifications of what *has* been done, written or spoken, not how to do it. About 2,400 years ago, the Greek philosopher-scholar Aristotle classified these forms or techniques, and he defined rhetoric as "finding the means of persuasion." Precisely. In the last analysis, most writing is *persuasion*—moving a reader to see, understand, and accept the meaning we intend.

The writing tasks that follow are not "assignments" in the usual sense. Rather, they are stated as writing problems. When possible, choose your own subject: something you care about or have genuine curiosity about. If you don't care, your writing will show it—ruthlessly. A *given* assignment may not interest you. But if you choose a topic for yourself, you have an investment in it.

The tasks are not intended to be accomplished in any special order. If you already write good descriptive paragraphs, choose another kind of problem. With the exception of the first three tasks, which should be kept to *one* paragraph, don't worry how long each should be. The only reasonable answer is: As long as necessary.

Many tasks are stated or implied in the first eleven chapters without much elaboration. Accompanying each of the following tasks are suggestions, reminders, and tips. These are intended as help from a silent editor-at-your-elbow.

TASK 1: DESCRIBE IT TO ME

In some ways, description is the easiest kind of writing. The information you need for describing a place or a person is already inside you or easily available. The scene or person is in front of you or in your immediate memory. You can look and see the details you need.

Writing descriptive paragraphs is a useful way to begin to develop the basic, crucial writing skill: your eye, ear, and instinct for the *specific*—for the concrete detail or example that *shows* your reader your meaning. (When I was a young writer, an editor said, "You're writing parallel to it, like railroad tracks. You're telling along one rail, and the reality is the other rail.")

Here's a warm-up exercise: Find a magazine picture of a scene without people in it. Look at it hard. What, exactly, are you seeing? Make a list of the facts of your observation. The list doesn't need to be in any special order; ordering comes later. It's important to get your facts into words as quickly as you can. Forget about grammar and spelling at this stage. You want raw material. Check your list against the picture. Are you telling *about* what you see, or does your list state precisely what *is* there? Do your notes say "beautiful lake"? or more specifically, "lake shore, sand, blue sky, film of white clouds . . ."? "Beautiful" does not *show* what you see.

Try a rough draft. The simplest way to begin is to say, "I am looking at a picture of . . . ." In later drafts, you will probably discard this first sentence, but it will get you started.

SUGGESTIONS

- Choose a point of focus or a dominant impression. Build your details from there.
- Cluster your details around the point. It isn't enough simply to list what you see from bottom to top or left to right. You want a reader to *see* a picture as you do. For instance, as I write this, I can see a painting of green hills. In a valley between the hills is a white church steeple. The steeple is the focus of the painting, though it is tiny compared to the hills. In a written description, I would choose details about the hills that radiate from the steeple.
- Apply these suggestions to a description of a person, too. We have first impressions of others: *big* guy (six foot seven); *pixieish* girl (small,

lively); *bushy* beard, *tall and skinny, precise way of speaking;* and so on. The impression can come from a mannerism: nervous tapping with a pencil, talking with hands, pulling at lower lip. In many ways, a person *is* as he or she acts. Focus on the impression; show the actions.

- Take a tip from the cartoonist or caricaturist. A caricature emphasizes and usually exaggerates a person's most visible physical characteristics: crooked nose, big smile (all teeth), thick eyebrows. A caricature or cartoon is, usually, unfair, precisely because of the exaggeration. But good cartoons have an unmistakable focus—and that's the reason for my suggestion.

- Where an *image* (simile or metaphor) is both apt and natural, use it:

> I dumped the cat from my lap. She squalled and raised her tail, showing the white button underneath. She stalked to the fireplace, *like a sneer walking,* and in one fluid motion curled up, tucked her front paws under her chest, and began to purr.

REMEMBER: A description should leave a reader with one dominant impression.

TASK 2: WHAT DOES THAT MEAN?

Every trade or profession has its jargon—its special language. There are times when you need to interpret this language to someone not familiar with it. A welder may want to explain to a customer what a *bead* is. A dentist, to inform his patient, may explain *calculus* and how it is removed from the teeth.

Mostly, such explanation tends to be visual: You want your reader to *see* meaning. The dictionary may help as a start, but dictionary definitions are often in terms of other terms, and the search can sometimes lead you in verbal circles. When you use a dictionary, pay special attention to the *root* of a word—where it came from. It's especially useful to understand prefixes. For example, when you read *dysfunctional,* you know that something is not working right: *dys-* tells you that. Or you find out that *hypo-* means "low" and *hyper-* means "high."

SUGGESTIONS

- Choose half a dozen terms that are special to your vocational or professional activity and explain them to an intelligent reader.
- When appropriate, use parentheses to put the brief meaning of technical terms in understandable language *within* a sentence: "*Plaque* (a gummy substance harboring bacteria) collects continuously on the teeth." "The injected drug *perfuses* (flows or spreads) under the skin or into an affected organ."
- Where you can, use images or comparisons. Remember that your obligation is to make the reader *see.*
- Your descriptive definitions may vary from a single sentence to a brief paragraph.

EXAMPLES

*Hypo*glycemia means abnormally low sugar in the blood. It's the opposite of diabetes. It means that the islets of Langerhans, tiny glandular nodules on the pancreas, are secreting too much natural insulin, and this is burning up blood sugar too rapidly.

*Hypo*thermia is a condition of literally freezing to death: The body temperature is abnormally low. Here, both prefix and word root help to understand it: *hypo-* means "low," and *thermē* is a Greek word meaning "heat."

(Sometimes, in cases of heart surgery, a patient's body temperature may temporarily be lowered by ice packs to a condition of hypothermia.)

Homeostasis is another term, usually medical or biological, in which the last part of the term tells the meaning: *stasis* means "stable." So homeostasis describes a system in balance: in a human body, a temperature of 98.6°F, blood chemistry (salts and acids) in proper proportion, and endocrine glands producing secretions in proper amounts.

TASK 3: EXPLAINING SPECIAL CONCEPTS

This is similar to Task 2, but potentially more challenging, which makes it especially appropriate because whenever possible, you should set yourself to writing tasks that can also be means of learning something new or clarifying and expanding what you think you already know. (Remember, writing is an exceedingly sharp learning tool.) For example, many students aim for careers in business, whether as entrepreneurs or as employees in a large corporate setting. One small but crucial key to success in such careers is a firm, accurate grasp of simple bookkeeping. (Many a small business has failed because the proprietors didn't have this working knowledge.)

Here are three basic accounting terms that are easy enough to define, but a thorough understanding of them is a complex matter indeed: *asset, liability, equity.* Using one paragraph for each term, explain the meanings simply and accurately. (Assume that your reader is an intelligent lay person who knows nothing about accounting.)

SUGGESTIONS

- In "translating" special terms into lay language, it is especially important to use brief, clear examples or illustrations. One "for instance" may be used to illustrate different applications of the same term, as: An *asset* may be real property, such as a building, that you own; the building may represent some aspect of *liability* (what you owe); it may also show an element of *equity* (what you've invested) at the same time. Or you may use three different examples to illustrate the terms. The writing task is to guide the reader into thinking of the examples as *accurate instances* of the general definitions.
- Don't assume previous knowledge by your reader. Lead the reader step by step toward understanding. Good explanations depend on a clear, logical sequence of statements, ideas, and, especially, examples.
- As an alternative, explain *double-entry bookkeeping.*

TASK 4: WRITING INSTRUCTIONS

Whether you write directions, or instructions about a process (such as how to operate a complex machine), your obligation to your reader is simple and clear: He or she must be able to follow your instructions without becoming confused.

SUGGESTIONS

- To the extent you can, know your audience. A person already skilled in the area your instructions cover needs less detailed information than someone who has little or no knowledge. A recipe is a good example. An inexperienced cook needs careful guidance, but a veteran cook may need only an ingredients list and the briefest of directions about what to do with them.
- List all the information a reader must know.
- Arrange this list in the order you expect your reader to follow.
- Write directly and simply.
- If needed for clarity, number or letter the instruction steps.
- When appropriate, emphasize the importance of a particular step.
- Define any technical terms the reader may not understand. Where you have any doubt, *over*explain. The reader needs to see clearly what you want him or her to do.
- Use simple diagrams if they will help.
- Test your instructions by following them yourself.

TASK 5: EXPRESSING AN OPINION

Most of us have strong opinions or feelings about all sorts of matters. "I can't stand smoke-filled rooms." "People who won't carry their share of a job ought to be fired." "There is nothing better than a cold beer on a hot day." "Children get their own way too much these days." "Most television is junk."

In one paragraph, state such an opinion of your own. I suggest the paragraph limit because it will force you to be tight and economical.

SUGGESTIONS

- Avoid emotional language. You may feel strongly, but overheated words fog up communication.
- Do not argue with anyone: You simply want to make your opinion clear. Avoid a scolding tone ("You should do this or that or the other").
- Be objective and factual. Two or three brief examples can make your point forcefully.
- Where you can, use your own experience for details you need.

ANATOMY OF AN INFORMAL ESSAY OF OPINION

When I was a young writer, I was especially helped by professional friends who showed me, step by step, how a nonfiction article developed from idea to publication. That same kind of journey might be useful to you, since it reflects some of the realities of writing for a nonacademic world. I'll set the context briefly for you.

Personal. I have just retired after thirty-five years of teaching writing and literature to undergraduates. For the first time in my life, I have full time to write. Several fat files of jottings, notes, ideas, and sources forecast enough work to keep me happily busy until I am 102. Maybe 104.

One of the most urgent "itches" I have to scratch is my angry awareness of the extent our schools are shortchanging—cheating—young students at all levels and my further awareness of how little the general public knows about the realities of this situation.

Further, I am in an atypical situation for a person my age (sixty-five and counting) of being solely responsible for bringing up a thirteen-year-old son. He is a bright, curious kid, and I am watching a reputed "good" public school drive him away from significant learning. I want to do something about that—anything I can.

Climate. Currently, the sociopolitical climate is right for public debate or discussion on education. Major national reports have deplored the ineffectiveness of our schools. In my home state (Maine), a governor's commission is viewing the situation with alarm. A national election year is coming up, and education is more and more an ingredient in the political stew. So the subject is newsworthy, and national and local publications are giving increased attention to it.

This has perked up my writer's instincts, and I have sketched out a series of five brief articles on aspects of the educational breakdown that I know of firsthand and that strike me as especially crucial. For me, the teaching and learning of writing had first priority.

Audience. Mainly middle- and upper-middle-class, with at least some college education, but including concerned parents at all economic and social levels. These are the people who are on school boards and parent-teacher committees or who are in positions to affect educational policies locally or statewide.

Medium. We have a statewide weekly newspaper that focused initially on environmental issues but has broadened its coverage in recent years to other social and cultural matters. Its subscribers and buyers are largely the people I mentioned under "Audience." The paper recently introduced a new regular feature, the *Maine Times* Essay, which, in the editor's words, "will be written both by staff and people not on the staff. It will be called an 'essay' to free it from the usual strictures of journalism, but it will be non-fiction. Subjects and lengths will vary, depending upon the desires of the author. . . ."

Building the article. The generating idea has been in my mind (and experience) for a long time, and it is the first sentence of the piece. The "answer" to the initial strong statement is the first sentence of the second paragraph. The development of the article had to be between these two boundaries.

Notice first that the piece is not in a single or "pure" rhetorical form. It is part persuasion or argument, part definition, part description, part brief analysis. As I wrote this, the notion of rhetorical form didn't enter my mind at all. My whole effort was to explain or support the two sentences I referred to earlier. In my mind *all* the time was the intended audience. Would my statements, examples, information ring true to my reader?

The article's beginning was a mess of 11½ pages of handwritten scribbles, phrase fragments, research quotes, asterisks, and scraps of typed notes. The first draft was 27 pages of double-spaced typing. What you read here was draft number 7: 5 pages of double-spaced material, or about 1,800 words. The hardest writing task of all was to simplify a complex subject without unfairly oversimplifying.

SUGGESTIONS

- Try to read this not as a student making an analysis but as a reader—perhaps one with a couple of kids in school, an employer who is fed up with employees' poor spelling and incoherent grammar, or a public official who may have some responsibility for the quality of local schools.
- As a reader, what particular statements, ideas, or examples caught your attention? kept your attention? What in the article was least persuasive?
- Whether you agree with my views or not, does the essay's central argument come across as reasonable, or at least considering?
- Go through the piece and cross out anything you feel is unnecessary.
- How would you characterize the "tone" of the piece?

Writing Cannot Be Taught, But It Can Be Learned*

A shocking number of American students—my estimate is at least 50 percent—are functionally illiterate, or nearly so: By age 18, they cannot write their native language with any clarity or precision. If they are increasingly tongue-tied on paper, they are likely to be tongue-tied in their heads. There is a connection. Then why don't our schools remedy this sorry situation?

The plain fact is that writing is hardly taught anymore in our schools at any level, including college. This statement may be taken as either irresponsible or preposterous. It is neither. It reflects educational misdirection on a scale so large that it is an open secret nobody talks about. To be sure, everybody *complains* about student illiteracy. The complaints have turned an educational problem into a political issue. This has in turn spawned the silly "back to basics" slogan and the inevitable nonsolutions that such slogans precipitate (such as the current vogue for "competency" tests). Despite public outcry and viewing with alarm, our students still don't learn to write, and the way things are going, they're not likely to. For instance, in the past twenty years I have worked with several thousand teachers of college writing, nationwide and in Canada. They consistently testify that each succeeding year, students

*This is a lightly edited version of an article published in the *Maine Times*, November 25, 1983.

who come to them have done less writing in the early grades and high school. Nowadays it is not unusual for college freshmen to have written *nothing* since seventh or eighth grade, sometimes even earlier. And it is possible to get through many colleges with fifteen weeks or less of writing instruction. If writing isn't being done, it isn't being learned.

Yet writing is perhaps the most powerful learning tool we have. The real "basics" in writing have little to do with grammar drill or usage exercises. The basics are at once more simple and more difficult, since they have to do with the way our minds work when we deal with information. "How do I know what I think until I say what I mean?" is not a flippant question; it's fundamental, because it reflects a potent way of learning. The single, overriding purpose of school should be to teach students *how to learn* in all kinds of situations, to give them the tools to keep on learning. Writing uses language to sort out meaning from experience and to organize and communicate that learning. The basics include the capacity to reason logically; to draw generalizations from particulars; to collect, evaluate, and organize evidence; to marshal an argument. The act of writing ruthlessly exposes vague, fuzzy, careless thinking. Perhaps this is why so many students—and teachers—avoid it.

Another element of the problem is the stubborn reality that writing cannot be taught, at least if we consider teaching to be "telling." It can, however, be learned. Like any skill, it must be done repeatedly, with steady, guiding feedback. *Writing is learned by writing, and in no other way.* No matter how skilled a person becomes, writing must always be relearned with every different attempt at expression. Most professionals will agree to this. Unlike speech, writing is an artificial act. It is the transfer into visual symbols what has been thought, experienced, felt, or observed. The transfer is tough, hard work. A student needs to know firsthand, as early and as often as possible, the sheer labor *and* the satisfaction of making into words what is truly in his or her head. (Significantly, the more accurately and fully a student knows what he or she is talking about, the more appropriate and correct his or her grammar and spelling will usually be.) The very process of hammering out meaning is the true "basic" of learning to write. "Writing is rewriting," said one fine writer. "It comes with the territory."

But in most schools, students are exposed to writing as a product, with certain formulas for producing it. This is called "English." They do little actual writing—composing—themselves. They hear and read and talk and do exercises *about* writing. Hundreds of textbooks, workbooks, "modules," and other devices prescribe, describe, demonstrate. (Most of them are in prose that is relentlessly stiff, colorless, and *dull*—though students discover this quickly enough.) Grammar is a set of rules: Do this and don't do that. Usage is displayed as sample essays, business letters, technical reports, and the like, to be examined and emulated for "proper form." Result: By the end of twelfth grade, students are scared witless of being "wrong." Every writing teacher knows the fatuous "Oh, you're an English teacher, so I'd better be careful what I say." This fear is real. It is probably the toughest barrier keeping ordinary, intelligent students from learning to write.

Teaching grammar, usage, and forms of rhetoric is not teaching writing. It is teaching linguistics, which is a subject, not a skill. As Pulitzer prizewinning writer Donald M. Murray aptly puts it, "It is as hard to imagine how writing is made from looking at the finished product as it is to imagine a pig from a sausage."

The teacher is at the center of this misdirection. I say this not in blame but in honest sorrow. Usually, English teachers have been trained in literature. Their college and graduate school writing has been in response to readings: words about words. As philosopher Alfred Whitehead wrote nearly sixty years ago, "What the learned world tends to offer is one secondhand scrap of information illustrating ideas from another secondhand scrap of information. The secondhandedness of the learned world is the secret of its mediocrity." Yet most writing in the "real world," as students put it, is *first*hand. Further, most teachers, believe it or not, had their last formal instruction in writing as college freshmen, in a course typically offering more reading than actual composition. And many instructors' first and only experiences teaching writing may have been as graduate teaching assistants with freshman sections. Typically, teaching assistants are given little guidance, though in most universities they teach a significant percentage of all freshman composition courses. "If the blind lead the blind," says the scripture, "both shall fall into the ditch."

A second correlative fact is that most teachers do little or no writing of any kind themselves. This includes college instructors. They do not practice the skill they presume to teach. If they don't practice it, they cannot truly know how writing is made or how it *feels* to students who are trying to learn how to make it. As a fair comparison, suppose you go to a dentist to have your teeth cleaned. Assume that the hygienist, who would normally do this routine task, read about tooth-cleaning in texts and manuals, discussed these procedures in class, and perhaps even scored 100 on true-or-false exams on the subject. But she has had no hands-on experience with the dental mirror or the explorers and curettes she is about to employ in your mouth. It is not far-fetched to suggest that a teacher who doesn't write is no more equipped to instruct that complex skill than the theory-trained hygienist is fit to clean your teeth.

So what's to be done?

The response is profoundly simple, and like most truly simple solutions, it could shake a lot of academic cages—and rattle more than a few textbook publishers. Start children writing *something* every day, beginning in second or third grade. For a very long time, the writing should be *only* from their direct experience or from subjects of their own interest. For an equal period, the writing should never (or rarely) be more than a brief paragraph. Indeed, in the early grades, even a couple of sentences a day would serve. The only criteria should be questions: "What, specifically, do you have to say? Are you saying it exactly, as you honestly mean it?"

From the beginning, teachers need to be, first and always, responsive readers. Students need an audience, not a judge. Teachers should not—repeat, *not*—"correct" everything. This would be a crushing and needless burden for them and a guarantee that their students would resist writing. Rather, teachers should gently, persistently, read and respond, insisting only that students be clear. If this is done, students learn to "correct" themselves. Such an approach could go a long way toward reducing the need for cumbersome, expensive remedial apparatus. (A fascinating aside: There is considerable evidence that the ability to code grammar and syntax is an innate, biological, genetically determined aptitude of the human brain. There is also evidence that mistaken school practices can distort or even suppress this aptitude.)

Let there be no misunderstanding. I am not suggesting that we replace our present failing system with some far-out practice based on highfalutin theories. I'm simply recognizing that our children have a skill to learn and that they should start learning it realistically as early as possible. Nor am I recommending in any way that teachers and students ignore grammar and accepted usage. Grammar is to language what the skeleton is to a body: the bones, the basic structure. Without a skeleton, a body would be merely a mass of tissue. Without grammar, language too would be shapeless, unable to express thinking adequately. But thinking comes first. As students are pushed to think clearly on paper, they will truly and functionally learn clear, unambiguous grammatical structure.

If day by day, year after year, we require our children to write briefly, and if they are rewarded for directness, honesty, and concreteness—not just for being "correct"—they *will* learn to write literately, just as (miraculously) they learned to talk. And there will be a special bonus: They will find their own individual voices. We could give them no greater gift.

TASK 6: ARGUMENT OR PERSUASION

When you write to argue or persuade, assume you have an opponent—
someone who disagrees with you. You want to change your opponent's
mind, as in a debate.

SUGGESTIONS

- State the opposing views briefly and fairly.
- Develop facts and instances that support your view. Be sure these sup-
  portive details are accurate. Check them if you need to.
- As always, let information do the work for you. *Never* use sarcasm or
  attempt to belittle or demean the person with the opposing view. Doing
  that will only guarantee resistance.

EXAMPLE

Recently, one of my students, a thirty-five-year-old woman with two children, brought me ten pages of yellow legal paper, scribbled tight. She
slapped the pages on my desk and said, tensely, "Read this." She and
other families in her neighborhood had been trying to get a school bus
stop shelter moved to a safer location. They'd had no success. Two days
before she saw me, her daughter had been hit by the school bus and
bumped into a snowbank. The child wasn't hurt, but the mother was
scared. I read what she had written. Then I said, "You're mad as the
devil."

"Damn right," she said. "And so is everybody in the neighborhood."

"What do you want to do with this?" I asked, pointing at the pages.

"Send it to the School Committee," she said.

I said, "I was a member of a school board for nine years, and I
wouldn't pay much attention to this."

She was outraged. "You *wouldn't?*"

"No, and I'll tell you why. You're so angry that you're incoherent. You
are abusive and name-calling. I can't be sure *what* you want. You even
contradicted yourself three times." She reached for the papers. I said,
"Wait a minute. Let me make practical suggestions. When did you plan
to present this to the School Committee?"

"In ten days," she said.

"Is this going to be a petition, signed by neighbors?"

"Yes."

"Then I suggest that you and your neighbors do these things: See the legal counsel for the school district, to determine liability. Talk to the dispatcher of the bus company about another and safer place to locate the stop. Find out the legal liability of the bus company. Talk to the police chief and legal counsel for the town. Get statements, quotes, from all of these people. Write up your petition again. First, state the problem as you and your neighbors see it. Tell, briefly, the incident with your daughter. Then cite the authorities you have interviewed. And bring me a draft."

Three days later she brought in a three-page statement. It was packed with facts and quotes and was logically ordered. The tone was objective. I said, "One thing is missing: What's your specific recommendation for a changed place for the bus stop?" She told me. I said, "Make that your last statement."

Her petition took the form of a memo. She told me the day after the School Committee met that the petition had been approved and that action would be taken as recommended.

When you argue or want to persuade, don't yell.

TASK 7: MAKING A PROPOSAL

The key writing problem is to give your reader information accurately and fairly so that he or she will make the decision you want.

SUGGESTIONS

- Tell the reader explicitly what decision you want. Come right out with it; don't try to be subtle or coy. (You've got to assume that your reader has as many brains as you have and is capable of making up his or her own mind.)
- Give the reader the reasons, in order of importance, why he or she should make the decision. Note that I say *reasons*—not rhetoric, emotion, or authoritarian commands.
- Quote or point to objective authorities to support your reasons and strengthen your case. In the absence of such authorities, assemble as many relevant *facts* as you can. (A fact is demonstrable; it can be proved or shown to be true. Something is not a fact just because you say it is.)
- It is perfectly acceptable to interject your own tentative conclusions or interpretations of facts. Just make sure that your information points logically to these judgments.
- Adopt a professional tone, logical and nonargumentative. Emotional or finger-wagging approaches may have an effective short-term result, but more often they either confuse the reader or provoke resistance.
- Physical presentation is important. As one editor put it, "Give the reader some breathing space." Often short two- or three-sentence paragraphs are clearer than long, packed ones.

REMEMBER: The reader has a decision to make—in the direction you want. So you must present information in the most open, attractive, and nonconfusing way possible.

TASK 8: DEVELOPING AN IDEA

Writing about ideas is something we are often called on to do: "Let's have your ideas on this subject." "What do you think of this idea?" "Explain your idea to me." In developing ideas, verbal barriers and pitfalls are many. Chief among them is the tendency to generalize about a generality, since ideas are often expressed in inclusive words or phrases. Dictionary definitions tend to be general. If, for example, you want to say something about freedom, you can be sidetracked by a loose trail of synonyms: *liberty, license, permission,* and the like. The synonyms are usually as inclusive as the idea-word you want to discuss.

Ideas *must* be related to the specific, concrete facts or circumstances from which they are derived.

There are several useful steps you can take to clarify or focus ideas.

1. *Identify or define.* In general terms, *what* is it that you are talking about? "I want to discuss discipline" (team spirit, enthusiasm, whatever).

2. *Classify.* Before you write, divide your subject into categories. Classify the idea of *power,* for instance, into *political* power, *personal* power (charisma), *physical* power (muscles, stength, stamina), or *mechanical* power (horsepower, pressure). Then discuss *one* category— or one category at a time.

3. *Contrast or compare.* Tell how your subject is like or unlike something else. If, for example, you want to develop the idea of aesthetic power or beauty, you might refer to Michelangelo's statue of David or to the Lincoln Memorial in Washington and compare those to other, lesser works. Such comparisons are, of course, personal judgments, and they are valid to the degree that you can make them specific and detailed.

4. *Find analogies.* Show that what you are explaining is *like* something which on the surface seems entirely different. For example, a certain musical passage may resemble (for you) the soaring flight of gulls or hawks. A good analogy is a powerful communicator. (It is not entirely far-fetched to assert that the central messages of Christianity derive from the analogies that Christ used in his parables and stories.)

5. *Use paradoxes.* A good paradox tickles the mind and stirs the imagination. A paradoxical statement seems to be a direct contradiction to what everyone assumes is factual or true; yet the paradox may have another kind of truth embedded in its very contrariness. "The meek

shall inherit the earth." "The most courageous soldiers I have known were scared all the time." "The more atomic bombs we build, the weaker we get." "The more he learned, the more stupid he got." "I am but poor in my possessions, my Lord; another richness is mine."
6. *Write for the senses.* In writing about ideas, it pays to remind yourself that we human beings have only five basic pathways of communication with the world we inhabit: sight, touch, hearing, taste, and smell. The more vividly and exactly we can relate an idea to one or more of these five senses, the more likely we are to communicate that idea as we want to.

SUGGESTION

Choose an idea, "concept," or feeling that can be expressed in one word, something that you have experienced fairly often. Let me suggest *delight.* It's a happy word, a lively word. It suggests greater than usual pleasure or satisfaction. But in itself, the word is vague, fuzzy. What "delights" you may bore another. The word has to be set in a context that tells a reader unmistakably what one or another specific delight means to you. Since delight is a quality of personal response to an experience, you need to relate, show, or dramatize a circumstance that produced the feeling in you.

Here is a one-paragraph example for you to examine. Ask yourself, first, "Does it communicate a sense of delight? What various *recognitions* does it stir in me?" Then go through the piece slowly and make a check mark at every point at which the writer engages one of your five senses.

Delight

The predawn was noisy with birds. In a sudden lull, a white-throated sparrow soloed like a tiny flute: "Old Sam Peabody-Peabody-Peabody." I smiled, waking, and rolled over, pushing the pillow under my cheek. The light in the room was a soft gray. On the bed table the clock face glimmered four o'clock. No need to get up yet. I heard in the hallway a series of light, rapid thumps; then a brief silence; then the door latch clicked. The door half-opened slowly. David, in a blue sleeper, clutching his stuffed puppy, stood for a moment in the opening. Then he ran to the bed. He climbed over me with little huffing grunts, wormed under the covers at my back, and wrestled the puppy over my face and down behind me. I turned and slid my arm under him, bringing his head to my shoulder. He lay still for a moment, warm and small. His blond hair had a light fragrance, like sun-warmed dry grass. "*Good* morning, Daddy," he said in his piping little-boy voice. "Did you have a good sleep?" He sounds like Old Sam Peabody, I thought: clear as a spring morning and just as welcome.

What a ritual of delight!

Though the *sound* sense predominates in this piece, all but one (taste) of the reader's senses have been called on. Also, you need to remember, as all writers must, that a reader brings his or her own *connotative* responses to the details presented. (Look up *connotation* once more. Often, what you connote is as important as what you state outright.) For instance, a parent reading this paragraph would automatically supply a train of association to the little kid climbing into bed. As a writer, you can foresee, and therefore provide for, many of these connotative clues or hints and thus enrich your communicating.

There are, of course, many other ways to discuss ideas; in all cases, substantive details, specific examples, illuminating comparisons need to be used. The usual route is from the general to the particular.

Suppose, for instance, you wished to discuss the idea of happiness in a somewhat more analytical fashion. You might begin with a definition, such as Edith Hamilton's in *The Greek Way:*

Happiness is the full and free use of your vital powers, along lines of excellence, in a life that gives them scope.

The definition suggests that happiness is *not* a destination or a fixed state but rather a by-product or accompaniment to activity. Roughly paraphrased, the definition says, "You'll be happy when you are free to give your full energy to doing your best at something you're good at." This is only slightly more specific than the original, but it clearly indicates that you need to be explicit about what "doing your best" and "something you're good at" refer to.

Some of my own happiest times have been in a canoe, in wilderness waters: slipping silently along a lake shore in gray dawn, watching deer and moose feed; or careening down a wild pitch of river white water, finding a channel among the rocks in the roar and foam. I am a skilled woodsman, and many months of my life have been comfortably, though sometimes strenuously, spent in primitive woods, a long, long way from telephones, supermarkets, and automobiles. The happiness from those months took its root from being, simply, free enough and capable enough to cope with elemental problems and find both comfort and excitement in them.

If you care enough about ideas—*your* ideas—you cannot hold back from exposing your feelings about them. If your writing ever gains power, these feelings become the sources and roots of its persuasion.

TASK 9: WORKING TO A DEADLINE

Much writing must be done within a time limit, both in school and at work. There is little or no time to revise. You have a memo to get out, a report is due, or you're writing an examination or quiz.

SUGGESTIONS

- Think before you write.
- Select one main point to make: a focus, or your primary point of view. If you have more than one point, put these in priority order.
- Make quick notes first. This will make the writing you do later go faster and more smoothly.
- Support each point with information or specific details. Sometimes a single good example or illustration can suffice.
- Don't worry about style. A brief, sharply stated piece is more persuasive than a sprawling one. Your response may feel staccato, abrupt. Don't worry about that. *What* you say in these deadline situations is more important than *how* you say it.

Examinations

True-or-False, Fill-in, or Multiple-Choice

- Scan the entire exam. Check-mark the questions you know the answers to; then answer them quickly.
- Go back to the questions you are uncertain about. Read each question again, to be sure you understand it. Then commit yourself to a response and forget it.
- If you have time before the exam period ends, go through your answers to check whether you have been careless. Carelessness has cost many a student grade points.

Essay

- Apply the suggestions above.
- Not all teachers know how to frame good exam questions. Before you go in to an essay exam, face the fact that it may be poorly phrased, or too inclusive for a one-hour or two-hour limit.

- Read the questions slowly, carefully. Underline the parts that seem to be most pertinent or important.
- Make quick notes.
- Within the time limit, try to set proportionate time for each question.
- Space and pace yourself. Leave a brief time at the end of the period to reread what you have written, and make corrections or brief additions.

HINT: The great mathematician Christian Gauss was once asked what he would do if he had to solve a problem in three minutes to save his life. He replied that he would spend two minutes thinking about it and one minute trying to solve it.

TASK 10: MAKING JUDGMENTS

We can't avoid the need to make judgments. In school and out, we are asked for *assessments, evaluations, analyses, conclusions.* (Before you go further, look up these four words in a dictionary and jot down definitions.) We may have to assess a program, evaluate a policy, analyze a procedure, or draw conclusions from evidence.

This can be a tough writing problem. You have to balance facts against expectations or criteria.

More often than not, our judgments are subjective responses—personal likes or dislikes—rather than objective assessments. We want to make our *feelings* known as clearly and persuasively as possible. The most important thing to recognize is that emotion-filled language usually does *not* communicate our feelings accurately. We have a large vocabulary of "heated" words and phrases: *wonderful, lousy, great, mean, dirty, stupid, lovely, happy, stinking, grungy, humongous,* and on and on. These words may reflect an attitude or state of mind, but they don't tell a reader much.

Currently, for example, there is wide controversy about smoking in public places: restaurants, aircraft, buses, elevators, and other places where people are close together. Nonsmokers claim (and there is research backing them) that "secondhand smoke" is almost as dangerous to their health as their own smoking would be. Often, however, much of their objection is less scientific than emotional or aesthetic. The way to write about these feelings is to identify or show their sources: lingering smoke smell in clothes or hair, watering eyes, irritated throat and nose, and the like. A reader is more likely to understand and accept your feelings when you *show* what causes them.

SUGGESTIONS

- State clearly and exactly what you are assessing or analyzing.
- Tell your reader the method you will use in this evaluation. Usually this means a statement of criteria.
- Help your reader think along with you. Lead step by step. If you want a reader to agree with your judgment, he or she has a right to know *how* you got to your conclusion.
- Take nothing for granted.

- If you are writing a favorable or unfavorable assessment, provide specific instances of performance or lack of it. Show what, where, and why (if known).
- If you are writing a proposal for action, tell your reader specifically, and first, what you want. Then tell why, giving reasons in order of importance. Document your reasons, where you can, with objective authorities.

Possible Tasks

- Make a value judgment, or more than one, of some happening or person. Or evaluate a mechanical appliance, a late-model car or truck, or an instance of unsatisfactory or slipshod service.
- Don't look at just one side: Consider both good and bad points, and balance them.

EXAMPLE

An abstract of a legal case can pose an interesting problem in analysis or judgment. Here is a summary of an actual court case on vicarious liability (second-person liability). Bridges is the plaintiff, the injured party. Willard is appealing a decision in favor of Bridges and against himself. The language quoted here is the language of the abstract; only names have been changed.

Bridges v. *Willard*

Appeal by defendant Willard from a judgment in favor of plaintiff for damages suffered by his automobile in a collision with an automobile owned by Willard and operated at the time by defendant Ogden. The evidence was that Ogden has asked Willard for permission to use his automobile for the purpose of taking him and his friend Johnson to a party. Ogden at the time displayed a quart of whiskey to Willard and told him they were going on a drinking party. Willard knew well that Ogden was in the habit of getting drunk. Ogden, intoxicated, drove the car at reckless speed on a zigzag course up a hill, and collided with the plaintiff's car.

The evidence clearly established that the car was being used solely for the pleasure of Ogden and Johnson. The jury returned a verdict against both defendants, and the court denied motions of judgment notwithstanding the verdict and for a new trial. . . .

The question presented for determination here is whether Willard, as the owner of the car, would be liable for damages caused by Ogden and

Johnson if, as alleged in the complaint, Willard knew or had reason to believe that Ogden and Johnson were incompetent or reckless persons to drive the car, or have it in their charge, and the circumstances were such that he was negligent in permitting them to take the car out upon that occasion.

The case went to the jury under instructions by his honor, the trial judge, that if Willard loaned the automobile with the intention or understanding that Ogden was to drive it, and with the knowledge that Ogden was likely to become under the influence of intoxicating liquors, he entrusted the automobile to Ogden in such circumstances as would produce in the mind of a reasonable man reasonable grounds for belief that the driver of the automobile might become intoxicated, and then in the event if Ogden is liable, Willard would be liable. . . .

We are inclined to the view that the trial court was correct as to the law of the case, and instructed the jury properly in that regard. . . . [Such personal] decision surely imposes upon owners some degree of care in the selection of experienced drivers for them. . . .

I have condensed this abstract only slightly, leaving out legal citations. But even that wasn't easy. The language is tangled and obscure; the references aren't at all clear—and this was a *simple* case. You can get the main thread: A man loaned his car to a friend who was a habitual drunk, after the friend had said plainly that he was going to a drinking party. Is the owner of the car liable for what his drunken friend did with it?

- There are ethical problems involved here. How far do the obligations of friendship go?
- Should Willard have said to Ogden: "No. You can't be trusted with a car"? How should he have handled the situation?
- Was the court's decision a fair placement of responsibility? Why?
- What about the passenger, Johnson? Did he have any responsibility?

SUGGESTION

- You may want to treat this abstract as an editing problem. The language is mixed up; references are not clear; and you read it wondering who is who. Try rewriting it so that a reader has no chance of confusion. You ought to get several pieces of writing out of this one.

TASK 11: WRITING LETTERS

Despite complaints that correspondence is a vanishing art, we all write letters. We reach out to a friend. We go on record with an opinion. We write to the editor. We praise, congratulate, or console. Here are suggestions to make your letters more effective than they may be now.

PERSONAL LETTERS

Say what you wish, of course, and in any fashion. (Few of us revise personal letters.) But remember that even a close friend wants to understand clearly *what* you are saying. As always, specific facts or examples are more interesting than wide-swinging generalizations. "That was a GREAT party, Charlie!!!" faintly conveys your enthusiasm. But Charlie might like to know *why* it was GREAT!!! so that he could do it again. Tuck in the odd fact or quirky observation. Even gossip is tastier when it is—or seems to be—factual. Anecdotes (little stories) are like raisins in a pudding.

BUSINESS LETTERS

A business letter is a matter of record. Always make a copy and keep it.

- Whenever you can, address a person by name and title.
- Be sure that your address, the date, and your telephone number (if appropriate) are on the letter.
- Begin your letter by stating immediately what it is about. If you are replying to a letter, refer to the date and subject. "This is in reply to your August 15 letter about . . ."
- Use facts. If your letter is about some failure or condition, state the situation briefly. "My clothes dryer is blowing hot air, but the tumble action does not work. My dryer is a—" (name the make and model number). A repair person will know that you need a new drive belt.
- Use typography to make yourself clear. If you have separate points, number or letter them.
- Write short paragraphs and sentences. In a business letter, the important thing is quick, accurate information.

LETTERS OF CONDOLENCE

Many people find condolence letters difficult to write. Remember: The important fact is that you wrote; you thought of the person receiving it. Keep it brief. If the event is a death in a friend's family, even if you knew the deceased well, your grief is not as pressing as the sorrow of the one who has lost a relative. "Dear Sue: I heard only yesterday of your father's death. I loved him, too, and I share your grief at his sudden passing. You are in my heart and thoughts." For now, that would be enough. You have touched hands with your friend, Sue, and it is the touching that she will be grateful for.

LETTERS OF RECOMMENDATION

Sometimes we are asked to recommend someone for a job, either by the person or by a prospective employer. It is not easy to make an assessment of someone else. Here are some guidelines and suggestions:

- Remember that *your* judgment is on the line. If you overpraise, for instance, you won't sound believable, and the person you recommend may not measure up to all the fine things you have said.
- If you have negative comments, by all means make them; often they will make an otherwise positive recommendation stronger. For example,

  Miss Jones is a first-rate organizer of other people's work. She is tactful and thoughtful and works well with others. However, because she is ambitious, she tends to take on more projects than she can handle. You will find, though, that she responds gracefully to supervision.

- State the person's strengths first, then the weaknesses, as you see them. These comments should be factual and explicit.
- Keep your tone calm and objective. Real praise will come through *what* you say, not how you say it.
- Any letter, personal or business, is *you*. Let yourself come through clearly.

SUGGESTIONS

- Write one or more of the types of letters outlined here. The circumstances should be real: Don't invent a situation.

- Write a letter to a friend telling specifically about a job that you have now. What does the job require of you? What are its major satisfactions? Its drawbacks? Do you think that the job has growth possibilities for you? Why?

TASK 12: WRITING A SPEECH

If you have to give a talk, it's smart to write it out ahead of time. Few people are skilled at extemporaneous speech. There are those horrible blank moments when you think, "What in hell do I say next?"

Speaking is different from writing. The ear takes in material less incisively than the eye, so a speech should be looser, more open, more repetitious than its equivalent in writing to be read.

SUGGESTIONS

- Use more anecdotes, illustrations, or examples than you would in writing. These enable the listener to "see" while hearing.
- Try to figure out your audience. Are the people out there your contemporaries? Are they of different ages and backgrounds from you? from each other? What *don't* they know that you have to tell them?
- List the number of main points you want to make—and don't make too many. Aural (hearing) memory is short. Be especially sure that you clearly link each point, even if you have to repeat yourself.
- Remember that you are having a conversation, though one-sided, with others.
- Talk slowly. What may seem hesitant to you will be natural pauses for listeners. (We tend to talk rapidly when we are nervous.)
- Use your voice pitch and strength to underline or emphasize a point.
- Above all, be yourself.

TASK 13: PUBLICITY

You may belong to a group that plans an event: a play, a debate, a game, or an exhibition. You want others to know about it so that they will come. If this is a school or college event, you may write a publicity release for the school paper. If the public is invited, you may write a notice for local newspapers or radio stations.

SUGGESTIONS

Here are some suggestions or directions that any editor would give a beginning reporter:

- Find out from local newspapers and radio stations what their cutoff dates are for accepting releases.
- Write a news lead. Tell *what* the event is, *who* sponsors or presents it, *when* it will occur (day and time), and *where*—a particular building, auditorium, or stadium. If tickets are needed, tell where these can be bought and at what price.
- Write what journalists call "short takes"—paragraphs of no more than four or five lines.
- Write simply. Your purpose is information, not graceful rhetoric.
- Names are important, especially for small-town newspapers and radio stations. For example, if the event is a play, name the director, stage manager, principal cast, and others closely associated with the production. This information should come *last* in your release.
- On the release, in an upper corner, give your organization's name and address, your name, and your telephone number. (An editor may want more information.) Also give the release date—the date by which you would like your story to be printed. (Your request may or may not be honored.)
- Take or send copies of your release to editors about a week ahead of the event. Write a follow-up release, with fresh facts, if this seems necessary.

And Here Are Some Don'ts

- Don't editorialize ("This worthwhile event, so important to many . . .").
- Don't exhort ("Let's get out there and support our team . . .").
- Don't inject yourself at all into the release. Use objective facts only.

COMMENT: Whether you are a publicity chairman or just the person who has to write releases, you will find it good practice to write objectively and logically. Be sure that you pick real events, about which you can get firsthand information. Get your information directly from participants whenever you can.

TASK 14: PERSONAL EXPLORATION

Many persons have a need to explore themselves: to clarify identity or personal standards or to rethink where they are. I have had many students who, at eighteen or nineteen, were beginning to explore what it is to be adult and others who, in middle age, needed to make a new assessment of their lives. One especially determined student, age fifty-eight, said, "I've had nine children. I'm a widow. I want to figure out where I go from here." The search is legitimate and healthy, and writing about it can help bring vague ideas or purposes into focus. The writing problem is how to be personal without being sloppy—how to express emotion, for instance, without writing incoherently.

Here are declarative statements, meant only to start your thinking. If you want to write in this territory, choose one or more statements to begin your exploration.

1. Above anything else, I am a person. I am me. I am the only me there is. I am the only me there is going to be. What I am, or become, is largely up to me.
2. I am female (male). In many ways, I am determined, directed, channeled by my biological makeup. How do I feel about this? Do I accept it? Nature cannot be fooled, and I am part of nature.
3. I am a social being. From my birth, I have related to others. I will relate to others until I die. What is the nature of my relating? In my relationships, am I still, freely, the person, the unique me? Or do I force another "me" as a price for getting along with others? (As T. S. Eliot said, do I "put on a face to meet the faces that I meet"?)
4. I am, or will be, a function: worker, parent, part of an economic and social fabric. Can the singular me survive being a function? I cannot escape a function role. What matters is whether I sacrifice myself to the function and become only what I do.
5. I need to believe that what I am and what I do are significant. But to whom? to what? Do I have basic beliefs (standards) that help me to respond to these questions? What are these beliefs? Are they vague or sentimental? Are they "religious" in the pious sense? Are they clear, firm guidelines for my decisions?

SUGGESTIONS

- Think about a decision you made recently, no matter how trivial. What were the circumstances of the decision? What standards guided you?

Having made it, what did the decision mean to you in personal or practical ways?

- Think about actual times when you refused to compromise your standards. Tell about those experiences, almost as stories or narratives. What did they cost you? What kind of cost? What was the reward?
- What are some personal qualities you respond to in persons you respect or love? Tell about these persons, or one person, to *show* these qualities.
- Think about a time in your life when everything seemed to "come together," no matter how fleetingly. Explain the feeling by being specific about the experience itself.

REMINDER: Our feelings or personal responses are usually triggered by particular circumstances or by the memory of them. The way to present those feelings is to write about the circumstances.

TASK 15: EXPLAINING A COMPLEX OR TECHNICAL MATTER

The chief writing problem is to simplify and to make the simplification clear to the reader.

SUGGESTIONS

- The more complex the subject, the simpler you should make the *sequence* of explanation. The key is *sequence*.
- Use short sentences during the key part of the simplification. If necessary, break your sentences into a numbered list. Give your reader *visual* space. Clarity is your aim, not style.
- Make any exceptions or qualifications clear.
- Briefly quote or refer to your major sources or authorities. In an informal article, you may do this in the body of the text. Use footnotes in a more formal paper.
- Use words that are as simple as possible. If you *must* use technical terms, define them immediately in parentheses or in the text.
- When appropriate, use simple diagrams or drawings.

REMEMBER: The reader knows the subject is complex; he or she needs all the help you can give to understand it. Remember how little *you* understood when you were first introduced to the subject.

TASK 16: USING THE FAMILIAR TO EXPLAIN THE UNFAMILIAR

Fine popularizers of science, a select group, have a special ability to use the familiar to explain the unfamiliar without oversimplifying the ideas they want you to understand. If you can learn to do this with difficult ideas or concepts—not just scientific ones—you will gain a valuable skill. A good explainer can see similarities among things that are apparently unlike, can link our knowledge or experience to matters that are new or strange to us. Aristotle said: "To link the known with the unknown—to make metaphor—is a sign of genius." I am not suggesting that you need to be a genius. But I am urging you to try to *explain* difficult ideas in terms of less difficult ones.

Your writing task is to select any (or all) of the terms and ideas in the essay that follows and to write an essay explaining or illustrating them with examples from your own experience or from everyone's common experience. The terms all have to do with ecology. Some terms are difficult. Though these terms are briefly explained, you should research them yourself. Use more than dictionary definitions.

Ecology (from Greek *oikos,* meaning "house or habitation," and *logy,* meaning "knowledge or study of") is the science of integrated biological systems. (*Integrated* means bringing parts into a whole.)

There are two basic ecological laws that we can't escape or evade, since they are the fundamental laws of our existence:

Ecological law 1: Everything is connected to everything else.

Ecological law 2: There is no free lunch.

The survival of life is based on diversity and adaptation. Only through the interaction of millions of species is *homeostasis* (stability) possible on our planet. The *food chain* of plants and animals connects the smallest marine single-cell organism to the most complex animal forms.

Our experience with the chemical DDT shows that DDT, introduced into the food chain as insect spray, can now be found in trace amounts in the tissues of almost every animal species—even in Antarctic penguins, who live thousands of miles from any DDT source. (We banned DDT in the 1960s. It's still with us.)

Thermodynamics (from Greek *themē,* "heat," and *dynamis,* "power") is a science that defines and interprets the relationships of energy, heat, and work. Energy = heat = work. Thermodynamic laws are universal.

First law of thermodynamics: Energy and matter can be neither created nor destroyed; they can only be transformed.

Second law of thermodynamics: Heat cannot pass spontaneously from one body to another at a higher temperature. (You can't make something hotter without expending energy—which means you can't do *anything* without an expenditure of energy.)

Energy is the source of all life. The ultimate source of all our energy is the sun. Fossil fuels—oil, coal, natural gas—are essentially stored forms of solar energy. The *biomass* (forests, grasses, peat, and other nonfossil resources) is likewise stored solar energy. Grains and vegetables are solar energy transformed by plants through *photosynthesis.* Meats are solar energy transformed by passage through the food chain from the smallest *phytoplankton* to complex animal forms. This is an example of the first ecological law. The first ecological law reflects the first law of thermodynamics.

The second ecological law reflects the second law of thermodynamics. It means, simply, that everything has an energy cost. *Nothing* can be done without expending energy. The result of the continual expenditure of energy is called *entropy.* (Entropy is a measure of disorder.) Whenever energy is expended, disorder increases, and hence entropy increases. Since nothing can happen unless energy is spent, entropy is always increasing.

EXAMPLES

If a house is not cleaned periodically, objects will be misplaced or lost (you use energy to move them; entropy increases). Result: Disorder (higher entropy), which will take even more energy to bring back to order (a further increase in entropy).

If you have a carefully tabulated list on cards, arranged in priority order, and then throw the cards to the floor, they will scatter in random order. The intact ordered cards represent a state of *low* entropy. Scattered, the cards are in a state of *higher* entropy. You would have to spend more energy to pick them up and sort them again.

It is also true that with the expenditure of energy we can create order. For example:

At high energy cost, we can change iron ore into a steel wrench. We have made a trade-off of the ore plus energy to make a useful object. In changing the ore to a wrench we expend energy and create a higher level of order (the wrench). But the *entropy* (total disorder) *of the universe* has increased because of the expenditure of energy.

In short, whenever *anything* happens, entropy increases. A price is always paid for every act and event. So we see why in the environment everything is intimately related to everything else (ecological law 1) and every action has a price paid in energy (ecological law 2).

SUGGESTIONS

- Try to understand as clearly as you can that energy is *the* payment we make for everything we have, including our own living bodies.
- Find and develop into at least several paragraphs examples from your own experience to explain, illustrate, or amplify some of the terms or generalizations made on these pages. Ask yourself questions: What is the sequence of events from a seed of corn in the ground, to a full ear of corn, to your eating of that ear, to your using the energy and excreting the residue? What happens to the residue?
- What happens when you burn a log in the fireplace? The log begins in a low-entropy state, but when heat (energy) is applied to it, the log burns and produces more heat. When the log is fully burned, it is ash— a state of higher entropy. Explain this process. (Rust [oxidation] is actually burning. A poet referred, accurately, to "the slow, smokeless burning of decay.")
- When you cook on an electric stove or turn on a light, where does the electricity come from? When you start a car, what happens? Low-entropy gasoline + spark = heat = work = velocity. What happens to the gasoline?

You should be able to find many examples in ordinary places and situations where you can trace the energy train.

The writing problem in explaining conceptual matters like these is mainly in finding appropriate examples or comparisons from familiar experience that do not distort or diminish the concept.

Additional Topics

- The size of the nucleus of an atom, compared to the whole atom, is about that of a bee in a cathedral.
- We can "see" the action of molecules without a microscope. A pan of water, at a rolling boil, is a collection of excited molecules.
- A nugget of gold the size of your little finger can be beaten into enough gold leaf to cover half a football field.

- The gold-weighing scale in the Central Federal Reserve Bank is so sensitive that it will decisively register the weight of a single pencil dot on a piece of paper.
- Einstein's theory of relativity states that light "bends" in the presence of a large celestial body. Imagine light as a blanket stretched taut, with a bowling ball in the middle, making the blanket sag.
- A leaf is a tiny manufacturing plant for turning sunlight and soil nutrients into food.
- A human being's visual system has more than a million channels capable of transmitting instantly ten million bits of information to the brain. Yet the brain has the capacity for receiving, at most, only twenty-seven bits of information per second. If the brain did not have the capacity to inhibit, or censor, these stimuli, we would instantly go mad. The inhibiting capacity is like a dam with one spillway: The backed-up water is contained and channeled.

Each of these topics is an example of comparing the unfamiliar with the familiar. We are familiar with the rolling boil of a pan of water, but we are not familiar with the idea that this ordinary sight lets us "see" a collection of "excited molecules." A cathedral or a large auditorium conveys a sense of size to most of us, but the size of an atomic nucleus, compared to the whole atom, is something we cannot "see" until a comparison is made.

As you try to make clear one or another aspect of energy, it is this kind of comparison you need to search for. If, for example, you choose to explore the generation of electricity by *hydro*power, the water pouring over falls or through dam spillways represents energy that you can literally see. Your writing task could be to trace the energy of falling water through turbines and generators to the electricity that makes the heating element on your stove glow red and transfer heat to the food you are cooking.

You will—always—need information to do this. Such information is abundant and not hard to find. Thus your *writing* about energy will once again be both exploration and discovery.

TASK 17: WRITING ABOUT WRITING

You are often asked to write about something you have read: a report, poem, essay, novel, or story. Writing about writing tends to be generalized, since it is secondhand—about reality once removed. However, there are useful ways for making your interpretations or criticisms sharp and interesting.

SUGGESTIONS

- Your first resource is your own response to what you have read. How do you feel about it? Did it teach you anything? Did it cause you to have a new awareness of the subject of the writing? Remember that what you read was written by someone who wanted to communicate with a reader—you.
- Decide what the writer's main point was. Do you agree with it? What are your reasons for agreeing or disagreeing? Use *brief,* specific quotes from the writer's material to show what you are commenting about.
- Try to characterize or summarize the subject of the writing. Then, as you discuss the piece and quote from it, your opinions will have a clear base.
- Three brief questions have been a useful critical framework for me ever since I first learned them as an undergraduate:

  What is the writer trying to say? (Summary)
  How well does the writer say it? (Aesthetic judgment)
  Is it *worth* saying? (Value judgment)

EXAMPLES

Here are two examples for you to work with. The first is a statement, a letter to a newspaper, by a Maine lobster fisherman about the possible impact of an oil refinery on the way of life in his area. He lives at the northeastern tip of the United States. He knows the sea intimately, as only a small-boat man can. Where he lives, the shore is craggy, with steep cliffs cut with narrow inlets. There are 35- to 45-foot tides (the highest in the world), savage currents, narrow channels, and an average of nearly 200 days of fog a year.

A lobsterman is one of the most independent workers in the world. He has his own boat, and he fishes when he pleases, as he pleases. This man's statement reflects his independence and self-reliance. (You'll be interested to know that he finished his formal education at the eighth grade.)

We are concerned people in this country. We like our clean, healthy outdoor life. Most of us own our own homes and lands, handed down to us by our fathers and grandfathers. Where else in the world can we find this? Not in industrialized cities. We are a self-employed lot. We aren't regulated by computers, except by the Almighty One which controls the winds and tides. We don't punch a time clock for five days a week, 51 weeks a year, and then maybe have a one-week vacation. We work where we wish, and as long as we wish, sometimes 100 hours a week. But *we* choose. Sure, our wages are low. But we don't spend thousands of dollars to find some place to hunt or go boating—we have it here. These same natural resources supplement our income. We all have gardens, with fresh vegetables and fruits to be canned. The air is clear and the sea is clean.

Yes, we have poor. Show me a town that does not have poor. Industry hasn't erased it. If anything, it has accentuated it. The poor get poorer and the rich get richer. But we have no starving, rat-infested ghettos here. One neighbor helps another. It has been proved time after time that industry will not lower taxes. They will rise. What happens then to our self-employed homeowners? They won't be able to pay these taxes. So goes our beautiful land, woods, ways of life, from our hands. Is this progress?

They talk of new conservation laws and regulations. These are good. But since when have we been able to teach the winds, tides, and rocks our laws? These are things involved in oil spills. Once oil is spilled here, what can the spillers say—they're sorry? The fish and wildlife don't understand sorry. They just die.

What we object to is oil—*here*. We don't want it coming in those mammoth 300,000-ton tankers into our dangerous rocky channels and stormridden tidal waters. These tankers are untried, untested, and unsafe. They are poor insurance risks. Why should we risk them?

We have fought the winds, the tides, the rocks, as our forefathers fought them for nearly 300 years. We don't wish our way of life to be wiped out in the name of progress.

This is a strong piece of special pleading. What is its special strength? Try to pinpoint it. Do you agree with the basic argument? Why (or why not)? Use examples of your own as contrast or support for your side.

Try writing a piece analyzing the statement, showing its chain of argument.

REMEMBER: Your strongest points are made by facts and by direct references to the source.

The second example, much different, is a poem. This poem by Robert Frost is a narrative, a story. It invites an emotional response. Feel free to give such a response. But again, be careful of emotional language. We speak best of emotion by showing its *sources*.

Out, Out—*

The buzz saw snarled and rattled in the yard
And made dust and dropped stove-lengths of wood,
Sweet-scented stuff when the breeze drew across it.
And from there, those that lifted eyes could count
Five mountain ranges one behind the other
Under the sunset far into Vermont.
And the saw snarled and rattled, snarled and rattled,
As it ran light, or had to bear a load.
And nothing happened: day was all but done.
Call it a day, I wish they might have said
To please the boy by giving him the half hour
That a boy counts so much saved from work.
His sister stood beside him in her apron
To tell them "Supper." At the word, the saw
Leaped out at the boy's hand, or seemed to leap—
He must have given the hand. However it was,
Neither refused the meeting. But the hand!
The boy's first outcry was a rueful laugh,
As he swung toward them holding up the hand
Half in appeal, but half as if to keep
The life from spilling. Then the boy saw all—
Since he was old enough to know, big boy
Doing a man's work, though a child at heart—
He saw all spoiled. "Don't let him cut my hand off—
The doctor when he comes. Don't let him, sister!"
So. But the hand was gone already.
The doctor put him in the dark of ether,
He lay and puffed his lips out with his breath.
And then—the watcher at his pulse took fright.
No one believed. They listened at his heart.
Little—less—nothing! and that ended it.
No more to build on there. And they, since they
Were not the one dead, turned to their affairs.

The poem's title comes from Shakespeare, from Macbeth's despairing cry:

Out, out, brief candle!
Life's but a walking shadow, a poor player
That struts and frets his hour upon the stage
And then is heard no more. It is a tale
Told by an idiot, full of sound and fury,
Signifying nothing.

This is potent, elemental stuff. The shocking suddenness of the accident to the boy; the linking of the title to Macbeth's "signifying nothing"—why did the poet do this to us? Is the boy's death "nothing"? Is it cruel, callous, to say, "And they, since they/Were not the one dead, turned to their affairs"? Is it enough for us to say, "Let the dead bury their dead"?

Or is there the implication that life must be lived, despite death in its midst? Is the poem a paradox that *affirms* life?

I have had nursing students, committed to nurturing and sustaining life, rage against this poem. "Dammit," one said to me recently, "don't these people *care*? He was just a kid—and then cut off, just like that."

What do *you* think? What's your gut response—first? Then, what is your more thoughtful response?

REMEMBER: Writing about writing means that you have to *go back into* the original writing itself. Quote it. Refer to specific passages. Base your comments on these.

TASK 18: WRITING POETRY

A poem can express a pure uprush of feeling or capture a fleeting insight far better than prose can. Poetry provides us with subtle resources of language and form that are often too elusive for plain statement. A poem is much more than a prettied-up way of saying something: It should be the best way to say that particular thing. It should make accessible to our understanding some awareness or feeling that may be lost in prose.

Poetry is instinctive in us. The voice of the human race was poetic long before it turned prosaic. Small children react instinctively to poetry; indeed, recent experiments show that children can write very good poetry indeed. That remarkable poet Dr. Seuss has introduced several generations to the magic of images and rhythmic language. So if you want to write a poem, you are responding to a deep and honest impulse rooted in thousands of years of your humanity.

Many poems "mean" in ways that are difficult to analyze; indeed, they resist analysis. Usually, we "talk around" a poem's meaning, since it cannot be rendered in prose. The poet arouses something in us—recollection, emotions, a fresh vision. Sometimes a poet will capture a striking image or series of images that convey meaning better than mere statement could. Ripples of awareness spread in our minds and feelings. A good poem *resonates:* Its aftereffects are like the sounding of a bell.

In a poet's characteristic way, Robert Frost described the phenomenon: "A poem begins in delight and ends in wisdom." Perhaps the delight is in the imagery itself—the pleasant shock of recognition—or in the sensuous sounds of word music. Shakespeare's incomparable line about young love, double-meaninged and metaphorical—"Oh, how this spring of love resembleth the uncertain glory of an April day!"—makes spring both a season and the quick assault of love at first sight. The dead-accurate matching of "uncertain glory" to describe April's weather is, simply, perfect.

Here is a brief poem by Robert Frost: °

Dust of Snow

The way a crow
Shook down on me
The dust of snow
From a hemlock tree
Has given my heart
A change of mood
And saved some part   (To *rue* is to be regretful,
Of a day I rued.   sorrowful, repentant)

There is, first, the visual image: the dust of snow. But there is, too, the implied contrast between the simple naturalness of the crow in the hemlock and a wasted day. It is as though the crow had said, "You've had a futile day at whatever you're doing, but I've reminded you of what is basic." The rhythm and sound of the little poem combine to lock the experience together: to focus our imagination. The exact reasons that poetic statement "works" in this way are not easy to determine. You may sense the difference if you contrast the poem with a flat prose version:

I felt snow falling on me. I looked up and saw that it was coming from a crow on a hemlock limb over my head. It gave me quite a lift, because I had been feeling depressed that day.

SUGGESTIONS

- If you want to write a poem, make an agreement with yourself that you will do a minimum of fifteen drafts. (Some poets do fifty.)
- Choose a brief happening (or emotion or insight) that stirred you deeply. Try to tell about the happening in a few prose sentences—not more than six. Write the sentences carefully, sharply.
- Try to find images: similes (using *like* or *as*) or metaphors that will evoke your meaning. A simile *states* that two things are alike. A metaphor *implies* a comparison. For example, a simile would say, "His hopes

°From *The Poetry of Robert Frost,* ed. Edward Connery Lathem (New York: Holt, Rinehart and Winston, 1969). Copyright 1916, 1923, © 1969 by Holt, Rinehart and Winston. Copyright 1944 by Robert Frost. Reprinted by permission of Holt, Rinehart and Winston, Publishers.

faded like the twilight." A metaphor would say, "The fading twilight of his hopes."

- Dig into your own experience, as deeply as you can, and match something in an experience with an image that seems to capture more than its literal meaning.

EXAMPLE

I have a couple of hundred acres of woodland. A century ago it was a farm. Now it is only a cellar hole in a pine forest. Deep in the forest is an old well, stone-lined, which I must clear every spring. Recently I suffered a grievous personal loss. The pain of this loss, at first, was close to unbearable, but as time passed I had to come to terms with my grief. I tried to express my feelings in a poem. I'm not sure the poem is much good, but it shows the way the mind has to work when shifting from prose to poetry.

Time Is Merciless with Grief

Time, the old healer, is gentle with sorrow.
Sorrow's tears are rivulets, quickly dried,
And sifted over with daily dust. But Grief:
Oh, Grief is loss, and time is merciless with Grief.
Grief is the old deep well,
Once brimming the clean stones
With cold sweet water.
Now the well is seeped away
To muck and sour moss and the husks of beetles.
The years cave in the well boards, and
Drop them, green-slimed, into the empty hole,
With rotted twigs and years' debris,
Until only the stones remember
The upwelling sweet cold water.

The emotions were made into metaphors: Sorrow is temporary rivulets, and grief, longer-lasting, is equated with the old well, gradually drying up and rotting.

Note always that the phrases and words bring pictures to the mind: *rivulets quickly dried, sifted over, brimming the clean stones, muck and sour moss,* and the rest.

REMEMBER: A poem is rarely a statement. It is a texture of images. It plucks at your heart before it hits your mind. In a poem, *every word counts*.

MORE POETRY

If you are a liberal arts student, or if you are taking a humanities course, you should be reading all sorts of provocative and wonderful stuff: drama, poetry, philosophy, essays. One good way to understand this reading is to try to *make* something like it yourself—no matter how far you may fall short of success. I have urged you previously to play with language. Here's an example of something you could try: a Shakespearean sonnet.

Shakespeare was one of many artists to commit themselves to a form. The rigid forms take enormous discipline, but they do have the advantage of pushing the artist toward focus and limitation and toward an effort to say, *within the form*, what is in both mind and heart.

A Shakespearean sonnet has fourteen lines, written in iambic pentameter. This means that each "foot," or *iamb*, sounds like this: *da–DA*. There are five (*penta*meter) feet in each line, so the rhythm goes *da–DA da–DA da–DA da–DA da–DA*. The rhyme scheme of the lines is *a b a b, c d c d, e f e f, g g*. Watch how it goes in a famous sonnet:

Let me not to the marriage of true *minds*	*a*
Admit impediments. Love is not *love*	*b*
Which alters when it alteration *finds,*	*a*
Or bends with the remover to *remove.*	*b*
O no, it is an ever-fixed *mark*	*c*
That looks on tempests and is never *shaken;*	*d*
It is the star to every wandering *bark,*	*c*
Whose worth's unknown, although his height be *taken.*	*d*
Love's not Time's fool, though rosy lips and *cheeks*	*e*
Within his bending sickle's compass *come;*	*f*
Love alters not with his brief hours and *weeks,*	*e*
But bears it out even to the edge of *doom.*	*f*
If this be error and upon me *proved,*	*g*
I never writ, nor no man ever *loved.*	*g*

As you read this, remember that Elizabethan pronunciation was different from ours, close to today's Irish brogue.

Writing a Shakespearean sonnet may seem impossible at first. You're no Shakespeare, after all. But—and it's a large *but*—I am asking you to play with language, to fumble with it, to make mistakes with it so that you can learn from it. It won't hurt you to have your mind stretched a bit by Shakespeare. He was, in case no one has told you, a *commercial* writer who learned his trade by working at it in a savagely competitive theater world. He was an actor, a part theater owner, and a writer of scripts on demand for his company. His early plays, with few glimmers of the brilliance to come, were pretentious and overblown. Of his thirty-five plays, he borrowed every plot but one, and that one (*Love's Labors Lost*) was a bright young man's mannered effort that probably would be a flop if written today. His only two long poems that were not plays were clichés, in the mode of his times. He learned his trade the hard way, the way most of us learn our trades.

So don't be put off by my request that you try a sonnet. You don't have to write of love, as Shakespeare did. *Any* subject will do, as long as you make a good try to fit the form. Your very attempt will be a success. I once had a dental hygiene student who wrote a sonnet to bubble gum. Her first line: "Let me not to the jointure of tooth and gum admit some Polident."

I gave her an A.

TASK 19: MAKE 'EM LAUGH

Except for poetry, humor is perhaps the most exacting kind of writing there is. Either it is just right, or it just sits there, soggy. If you know stories or anecdotes that have been handed down in your family or regional stories that seem to belong to everyone or personal experiences that have seemed genuinely funny to you, perhaps you'd like to take a risk and try a humorous story.

I'm not going to try to define humor. That would kill it. But there are characteristics worth comment. These may be useful, may spark you to try your hand at a funny piece.

We laugh most heartily at what is ludicrous in ourselves and in our situations. Our follies and vices are prime targets. The vain, pompous person falls abruptly on his butt. The silly, pretentious person gets cut down to size. The sly schemer is undone by his own cleverness. Folk tales of every culture often have such moral lessons in comic form. Fables are rich sources of thoughtful laughter. (Read Aesop, for instance.)

Much humor, anywhere in the world, has solid regional roots. The rural bumpkin versus the city slicker is universal. In the United States, the expansive western plains and mountains seemed to spawn tall tales, the big brag, and slap-'em-on-the-back stories. The South has produced wonderful, leisurely stories with intricate details and side comments. There is no better example than Mark Twain's *Jumping Frog of Calaveras County.* Yankee humor, perhaps because of the spare, hard country and the relentless winters, is apt to be compressed, dry, astringent, understated. The Texas rancher brags to a Yankee friend, "Why, ol' buddy, mah rayunch is so goldurned big it takes two days to drive around just two sides of it!" and the Yankee replies, "Ayeh, I had a car like that once."

The best humorous writing is specific, visual, circumstantial, believable. At the end of the tale, there is usually a "snapper"—an abrupt and realistic reversal of what we have expected.

SUGGESTIONS

- Keep a humorous anecdote tight, moving along. Don't ramble, and especially keep your sequence clear. There's the story of a young minister, fresh from the seminary, eager and conscientious, who is circuit-riding the small towns of New England, each with its church, but each of these too small to support a full-time pastor. In one town, the preacher found that his entire congregation was one old farmer. He asked the old man if they should have a Sunday service. The farmer thought for a bit, then replied, "Well, Reverend, if I put some hay in the wagon and went to the pasture to feed the cows and only one cow showed up, I'd feed her." So the preacher did a full service: hymns, responsive reading, scripture, full-length sermon, and long benediction. Afterward, he asked the lone congregation member what he thought of it. "Well, Reverend, if I had a full wagonload of hay and only one cow, I wouldn't feed her the whole damn load."

Don't give your reader the whole damn load.

- The tendency today, reinforced by television, is to "one-liners"—response in a matter of seconds. This is not humor; it is instant gratification, and it spoils real comedy. Humor, like good wine, takes a little time to ripen. Even a short anecdote should establish a feeling of persons and place before the inevitable switch.

- If you tell a story in which you were involved, give your reader time to get into it; build the details. Don't rush it, and don't start giggling at your own joke before you're half through. Tell it straight.

My favorite experience was when I was a teenager, learning to be a professional guide to take "sports" into the northern wilderness on long canoe trips. My teacher was Ed Dunham, a hearty, woods-wise man, who had spent most of his life cruising the rivers, lakes, and forests. On one three-week trip, after the second day, he said casually to us, "I can't see why you fellers want to heat water for shavin'. I can't wait to get to my 'lectric spruce on Eagle Lake. Get me a good shave then with my 'lectric razor." The sports groaned and said, "Aw, c'mon, Ed, there's no such thing as an electric spruce." Ed smiled, slurped his coffee, and said, "You fellers out of the city just don't know nawthin' about the wonders of nature. Find some purty damn interestin' stuff in the deep woods." As each day passed and we got closer to Eagle Lake, Ed's beard would be scruffier, and he'd keep saying, "Won't be long 'til I get to my 'lectric spruce and git a shave."

We got to Eagle Lake and a fine campsite. We set up tent flies and organized dinner. Then Ed said, elaborately casual, "Wal, I think I'll go to my 'lectric spruce and git me a comf'tble shave," and he made much business of digging into his pack and showing an electric shaver, with the cord dangling. He walked slowly toward the fringe of trees and stopped before an enormous blue spruce. His broad back was turned to us, and we couldn't see what he was doing. Suddenly, there was a loud buzz, and Ed was guiding the shaver over his stubbled cheek. We rushed to see. The cord simply disappeared into the branches and seemed to be plugged into the trunk. "Honest to God, he *meant* it!" said one of the sports. Ed laughed and wheezed and said, "I *told* you there was cussed miracles in the woods." The shaver buzzed on.

Later he told us that on his first trip in the early spring, he had gouged a deep recess in the spruce trunk, installed batteries and an outlet, and then put back the cleverly cut bark surface so that the tree trunk would look undisturbed. Still wheezing, he said, "God, suppose I'd 'a tried to sell you fellers some gold mine stock. My, oh my, I'd 'a got rich."

There was much mileage in that practical joke, and a lot of it came from Ed's comment, "My Lord, people is so damn gullible, it's fun to tickle 'em along."

■ Humor can also instruct, gently. A story I heard when I was a boy has stuck with me for half a century. A tourist stopped at a country store. Four old men were sitting on the steps, whittling. The tourist tried pleasantly to make conversation. He couldn't get a word out of them. Slightly irritated, he asked if there was a law against talking. One old gentleman said, "No, there ain't no law 'gainst talkin'. But we keep our mouths shut unless we're damn sure we can improve on the silence."

■ Test your editing skills on these two brief stories, both academic favorites of mine. Can you write either one any tighter? What would you change to make each one better?

On the Cornell University campus there's the story of a Professor Corson, who strode about looking as if he had emerged from the Old Testament. He wore a long gray beard and a long frock coat, and he would take great strides in the manner of Jeremiah or Joshua. One day, so the story goes, a couple of smart-sassy freshmen decided to "fix" the professor. The first interrupted his walk, bowed deeply, and said, "Good morning, Father Abraham." The second also bowed, saying, "Good morning, Father Isaac." Professor Corson drew himself to his considerable height, glanced scornfully down at the two freshmen, and said in rolling tones, "I am neither Father Abraham nor Father Isaac. I am Saul, the son of Kish, out looking for my father's asses—and lo! I have found them."

The other story has to do with a gentle, absent-minded professor of philosophy.

He was awakened by his phone ringing at 3 A.M. He struggled to the phone, and the voice of an irate neighbor complained bitterly that the professor's dog had been barking without stopping since early that evening. And, the neighbor snarled, would the professor please shut up "that damned dog." In the tradition of gentle forbearance, the professor waited until the next night, when he set his alarm for 3 A.M. He staggered to the phone, rang his neighbor's number, and when the neighbor finally answered, announced, "Madam, I have no damn dog."

Funny things happen to us, or we remember favorite jokes. They deserve telling. Go ahead, try one. "Did I tell you about the time—?"

TASK 20: VOCABULARY BUILDING

Most so-called vocabulary-building exercises are of little or no help be-cause they don't ask you to work with words whose meanings you *need* to know, the need coming from the context of your daily work.

There are two excellent ways to increase your functioning vocabulary. One is to learn the special language of a new activity, whether it is work or leisure. For example, if you learn to sail a boat, you have an immediate need to understand *tiller, sheet, chine, leeboard, luff, jibe, tack, halyard,* and so on.

The second is almost a game. When in the course of your job or your schoolwork, jot down words that are *not* jargon or technical terms and play with these. I mean *play.* (Numbers of my students have confessed that they actually enjoyed the game that I'm suggesting.)

Take these steps:

1. Look the word up in your dictionary. Be sure that you understand not only the primary meaning but also the roots, the obsolete meanings (if there are any), and the secondary or connotative meanings.
2. Try to invent an *image* (simile or metaphor) or an appropriate *comparison* to illuminate or associate the word's meaning. Don't worry if your images or comparisons are occasionally far-fetched or odd; that's part of the fun.
3. Try several phrases or images for the same word.

For example, when the French writer Jean-Paul Sartre was asked, "What is hell?" he replied with a metaphor: "Hell is other people." (Cynical but vivid!)

One of my students ran across this one in her reading: *hiatus.* The dictionary indicated that *hiatus* meant "a break, a gap, a lapse or inter-ruption." She asked herself: "A hiatus is *like*—what?" And she came up with "like parentheses with a blank between them: (   )." Not bad— good, in fact, especially with the visual blank between the parentheses.

You must, of course, come up with the words that *you* meet and need to know about. Here is a partial list that one group of students found in one day of doing homework:

febrile	arbitrate	evanescent	mandate	sentient
slovenly	assimilate	exacerbate	symbiosis	synergy
mediate	ancillary	frivolous	plurality	majority

As always, these are simply to get you started. And this time, there is a guarantee: If you take this game seriously, you will never forget the words you played with.

chapter 13

To Write
Is to Learn

Writing *is* learning. The more you use writing, in school and out, the more surely you will learn what you need to know in any area. The reason is simple. Writing is an act of pulling together, of making pieces of information coherent, of presenting examples that illuminate the information. It is a way of finding the *relatedness* of apparently unrelated facts. People who have this skill of expression are people you listen to, respond to—and learn from. The process of writing reveals how much or how little you truly know and how much you have yet to understand. If you know it, you can write it. It's put up or shut up. Whatever your problems or the challenges to your abilities, it pays to *write them out.*

To write is to develop an especially effective method of *thinking.* Many people have peculiar notions about what "thinking" is. They picture, perhaps, the brilliant TV private detective on a murder case who, with point-by-point logic, sums up evidence and accuses the butler of the killing. Or they envision Rodin's famous statue of the seated man, chin on fist, staring into space. Or they think of the white-coated scientist, alone in his laboratory, creating breakthrough experiments.

All this is nonsense. Thinking is the way we respond to a problem, the way we *act* in the face of it. It is what we *do* with what we know. An ancient Jewish assertion says, "Wisdom is essentially intelligent activity—knowledge suffused into action." That is a profound statement, worth pondering.

The act of writing is an act of thinking. Most real thinking is an exploratory process, tentative and groping. So is writing. To *think* is first to be curious. Too often we are fixated on answers. But there is nothing more irrelevant than the answer to a question that nobody asks. The real thinker, no matter who or how well educated, asks not only *what* but *why*. When you write, you ask why. Why this fact instead of that? Why this example instead of another? Why this phrase or that word? As you write, you search for meaning, for understanding, and the root question behind meaning is always *Why?*

This is precisely why writing is such a sharp learning tool, much like a surgeon's scalpel. *You work your way into thinking,* the way a surgeon works his way into a body: cut by cut. If you could listen, as I have, to a surgeon's recorded comments as he does an exploratory operation, you would understand exactly what I mean. "We have a mass here below the spleen, about five centimeters broad. We'll have to excise the mass to find its depth and whether it has spread or is isolated. We'll need immediate biopsy of the tissue mass. . . ." *Exploratory* again. Looking. Learning.

Like writing, thinking is not fixed or formulated. It is activity.

The philosopher A. N. Whitehead said, "If you want to understand something, make it yourself." Confucius, Chinese sage, said, "I hear and I forget. I see and I remember. I *do* and I understand." Sophocles, Greek dramatist, said, "One must learn by doing the thing, for though you think you know it, you have no certainty until you try." Auguste Rodin, sculptor, said, "Make something, and the idea will come." These are short, useful definitions of learning—and thinking.

When you write, you *do* and *make.*

Here are two brief instances, one of a student who *masked* with language his lack of understanding, the other a student who used language and experience to *reveal* her understanding. The students had been asked to explain briefly one of three related (though different) terms: *illusion, mirage,* and *hallucination.* The first student wrote:

The dictionary says that an illusion is an "unreal or misleading image, a deceptive appearance, a false impression, or a misconception." A man in ragged clothes was staggering across the burning desert. The blinding sun beat down on his uncovered head. His canteen was empty. His tongue was swollen and hanging out. Suddenly, he saw in front of him a blue lake and green trees. He began to run toward it, gasping for breath, but it kept moving away from him and finally disappeared. It was only an illusion.

This writer wasn't thinking; he was just putting together words that he thought meant something. He'd seen too many TV shows. The writing is phony and labored; the situation is a cliché. The writer admitted that he'd never seen a desert; never been agonizingly thirsty; never seen a *mirage* (not an "illusion")—and his writing shows it.

Contrast his writing with that of another student:

All morning I was in the library. I sat near a window. I could see grass and trees green with spring. In the little parking lot just below the window was a Volkswagen. It was polished and shone in the sun. As I looked at it, a robin hopped up to one wheel, cocked its head, and jumped up to peck at the hubcap. He jumped up, pecked, cocked his head, and jumped again. He hopped away a little, then came back to peck again. I realized that he must have seen his image reflected in the shiny hubcap—another robin on his territory. I do not know whether this was mating or combat. But the bird kept it up as though the reflected robin were a real adversary. Finally, he hopped away into the grass. It made me think that maybe human beings are not the only ones who act on an illusion as though it were real.

The second writer was *thinking:* She made a relationship between a concept ("illusion") and her own real observation. It's the reality—the honesty—of the connection that is important.

In school, the function of papers and essay exams is to ask you not only to tell what you know but also to show the extent of your grasp of the relationships of facts and ideas. In many ways, learning is weaving a web of understanding, one strand at a time. Language is a tool to help you explore facts and find understanding.

Suppose you are asked in a humanities course to explore the idea of romance or romanticism. The dictionary won't tell you much. It suggests that romance concerns feelings and imagination, rather than strict reality or objective analysis. There are echoes of love and adventure. Definition is not simple. But there are examples, hundreds of them, in music, visual art, literature of all kinds. Do these examples have qualities in common? Can you characterize these qualities? As your questions lead you deeper into romantic territory, you accumulate illustrations: a novel by Charlotte Brontë; Shakespeare's sonnets or *Romeo and Juliet;* poems of Wordsworth, Keats, Byron, Shelley; songs of Schumann or Mendelssohn; paintings by Delacroix or Constable; a play by Friedrich Schiller.

As you read or listen or see, you make note of your own responses and accumulate short, appropriate quotations. You read critical appraisals of poets, novelists, and artists and of the cultural context in which they worked. You begin to sense how currents of ideas affect the production of artistic works of all kinds. You learn that although "romanticism" is a label for a certain period of the nineteenth century, that what is "romantic" has been a thread in art from the poems of Catullus (Roman) and Sappho (Greek) to modern gothic novels. This is your information. Using it, you can begin to write your way—think your way—into an understanding of the concept of romanticism.

As you read the preceding paragraph, you may have been shocked by the amount of reading and research it suggests. Indeed it does suggest work—plenty of it. If you want an *education,* not just a piece of paper that certifies that you have provided a lot of textbook answers, *the work comes with the territory.* A real education is proved by what you can *do* with what you are supposed to have learned. Real learning is an adventure—and adventure means exploration, risk, and commitment. Like anything else worth getting, it doesn't come easy.

WRITING TO CLEAR YOUR MIND

In our out-of-school lives, difficult problems or decisions can be faced realistically by writing down the known facts, as opposed to guesses. For instance, one of the major financial decisions many people face is buying a house or renting an apartment. It would be foolish to make this commitment carelessly or haphazardly. Exactly what resources do you have that you can count on? What further resources can you find—a mortgage? At what rate and for how long? What is the structural condition of the house you want to buy—beams, roof, plumbing, heating system? The questions multiply. You can make an informed decision by writing down, as precisely as possible, answers to such questions. Most important, the writing itself will invariably stimulate additional and possibly crucial questions you may have overlooked.

You can use the writing-learning tool for personal decisions, too. I had a student recently (I've had many like her) who was being pressed by a young man to marry him. She thought she loved him, but she had reservations, and she wanted comment from me. Instead of commenting, I suggested that she write specific examples of his behavior in as many different circumstances as she knew. A week later, she brought me more than a dozen short paragraphs. Her young man invariably got drunk at parties, often to her acute embarrassment. When he had a problem at work, he got smashed before he went home. He continually borrowed from friends and paid back only sporadically. He was behind in his car payments. He was, apparently, charming and good company, *but*—as the student could see after having written out her profile—an immature person who postponed his own problem solving by leaning on others: not a good bet for a lasting relationship.

I don't suggest by this last example that writing can be do-it-yourself psychiatry—though I have seen it have good therapeutic effects. Honest, specific writing is a way of seeing reality clearly—and thus is a way of thinking and learning.

GRADE YOURSELF

A typical, and legitimate, student question is, "How do I get a good grade?" The descriptive list here is a consensus of nearly 500 college writing teachers who, in professional workshops over a number of years, were asked to respond to the question: "What is an *A* paper? *B*? *C*? *D*? (If it comforts you any, *all* of the teachers found the question stubbornly difficult, and agreement was both painful and slow.)

An *A* Paper

- An *A* paper conveys immediately a sense of person behind the words; an individual voice speaks firmly and clearly from the page.
- The title and lead sentences work smoothly to indicate the direction, scope, and tone of the whole piece. The reader feels the writer's assurance and is in no doubt about what is being communicated.
- The writing is packed with information. Examples or comparisons are carefully chosen and have a "just right" feel to them. Occasionally there is a vivid image or deft comparison.
- Organization of material is logical, clearly developed. The reader does not stumble or hesitate over the sequence of facts and ideas. Transitions from one point to another are smooth, almost imperceptible.
- Sentences are varied, with rhythms and emphasis suited to the meaning. Phrasing is often fluent and graceful. Sentences read well aloud.
- Word choices, especially verbs, are accurate, sensitive to connotations. There is an absence of "clutter"—heavy or hackneyed expressions used instead of a short word that means the same thing.

- Punctuation is appropriate, giving the reader helpful or necessary signposts for pauses and stops.
- There are no mechanical errors (grammar and spelling).

An *A* paper is not flawless; there is no such thing in writing. But it reflects a writer who is in full control of both material and language. *Control* is the key word here: The reader feels expert guidance.

A *B* Paper

A *B* paper has the characteristics of an *A* paper, with the following flaws:

- Information may be thin. The reader wants—*needs*—more. Examples or illustrations may feel slightly forced or exaggerated.
- Organization is clear; the reader does not confuse the sequence of information or ideas. However, transitions (especially between paragraphs) may be awkward or abrupt.
- Sentences tend to be of similar structure and are occasionally awkward or wordy. Relative clauses may be poorly placed.
- Word choices are workable and clear, though verbs may lack bite or strength.
- Punctuation is occasionally confusing.

A *C* Paper

- A *C* paper is characterized by awkwardness throughout. It does not read smoothly aloud.
- Information tends to be adequate, but barely sufficient for clarity.
- Organization is occasionally confused, especially between sentences. The reader sometimes has to stop and reread material to be sure of its meaning.
- Sentences have little or no structural variety. Phrases are often awkwardly placed. (Modifiers, especially adverbs, are sometimes too far from the word they modify.)
- Diction is usually characterized by wordiness and clichés. Unnecessary words and phrases make the writing loose.
- There are several grammar, spelling, and punctuation errors.

A *C* paper will do: It's adequate. But it gives the reader an impression of fuzziness and lack of assurance on the part of the writer. The reader has to *work* to understand what he or she is reading.

A *D* paper

- The main impression is one of haste, carelessness, lack of attention, or simply an inability to draft even direct or simple statements.
- The paper may make some sense, but only if the reader struggles to find it. The writer obviously has scanty control of the material.
- There are numerous structural and spelling errors, and the visual presentation is sloppy.

A FINAL WORD

If you accept no other advice in this book, you'll profit most by following this: *Get it down!* Fast, fuzzy, vague, sloppy, disorderly, mixed-up, confused—it doesn't matter. Just get it on paper. Then work with it, build it, shape it, tinker with it. Finally, make a piece of writing of it.

Trust your own responses, your hunches, your instinctive feel of rightness. It is the way to honest writing, to the clear saying of what you truly mean. It is the way to speak on paper in your own unmistakable voice.

Index of Tasks, Problems, and Assignments

As you have doubtless gathered, I believe that a significant first step in a writer's job is the personal selection of subject or topic. But many people who have used this book have been kind enough to provide some feedback. One persistent comment: "We confess that we're used to assignments, and it would help if you would provide more of them."

Though Chapter 12 sets out a good number of suggested assignments, there are nearly fifty more embedded in the preceding chapters, where writing tasks are stated or are implied in the text.

Here is an informal index, loosely classified according to type of writing problems or possible assignments. The aim of the index is to help you make choices of tasks that could be appropriate to your stage of learning—or, better, that provoke your interest and curiosity.